Captain Cobwebb's Cobr

Also in Armada by Gordon Boshell

Captain Cobwebb
Captain Cobwebb's Cowboys
Captain Cobwebb's Adventurers

More Captain Cobwebb titles will be published in Armada shortly

Captain Cobwebb's Cobra

Gordon Boshell

Illustrated by Graham Thompson

Armada

First published in 1971 by Chatto & Windus. This edition first published in Armada in 1977 by Fontana Paperbacks, 14 St. James's Place, London SW1A 1PF.

Printed in Great Britain by Love & Malcomson Ltd., Brighton Road, Redhill, Surrey.

CONTENTS

CHAPTER 1

ENCOUNTER IN THE MIST

ONE day at lunch Mr Green said, 'David . . . Toby . . . listen to me. Your mother and I are going up to Town this afternoon to visit Aunt Christabel in hospital. Now don't get into mischief while we are away. We shall be back by early evening.'

Mrs Green said, 'There are some chocolate biscuits in the blue tin in the pantry . . .'

'Oh, good!' mumbled Toby, who enjoys food—almost any kind of food.

'. . . And don't talk with your mouth full, Toby,' said Mrs Green. 'Those biscuits have to last a week, so don't make a pig of yourself. As for you, David,' she went on. 'if you intend to play soldiers again, don't go using my potatoes for cannon-balls like you did before.'

'Can we have some fizzy water?' asked David (he loves the tingle on his tongue).

'You'll find two bottles of lemonade in the refrigerator,' answered Mrs Green, and Mr Green broke in, 'And I don't want a repetition of what happened last time—shaking the bottles and then spraying the stuff all over each other—*and* the kitchen ceiling.'

'We won't spoil the ceiling again,' said David, thinking how odd it was that when you get two grown-ups together they so often go on saying the same kind of thing.

'Anyway,' added Toby consolingly, 'lemonade's no good for squirting. It hasn't got enough fizz.'

'Cherry Sparkle is better,' said David.

'It's a *bit* better,' agreed Toby, 'but Ice-Cream Soda's best. You've got to shake the bottle really hard and hold it just like this,' he went on enthusiastically, and he grabbed the bottle of Mr Green's favourite sauce and shook it vigorously . . . and the top came off and the sauce came out and of course (what else could you expect?) it shot all over the front of Mr Green's white shirt and ran down in great crimson blobs.

'Ooooh!' whispered Toby.

'Ah . . . ah . . . AH!' began Mr Green, wildly.

But David was too excited to notice that 'Ah . . . ah . . . AH!'

'Toby. Toby, look at it!' he cried. 'That's just what we need when we're playing at soldiers—tomato ketchup! It makes *smashing* blood! Just look at it!'

And then Mrs Green was saying loudly, 'DAVID!! . . . TOBY!!!' By now Mr Green reached the loudest 'AH' that he could and he raised his arms in the air and called, 'Out . . . *out* . . . OUT! Get them out! How dare we go away, even for a few hours, and leave those children in the house?' he asked Mrs Green. And she declared, 'I shouldn't have a moment's peace.'

'Then give them their biscuits and their lemonade,' said Mr Green 'and send them *out* to play. I shall lock the door when they go and they shall not come into the house until we're back.'

So off went Mr and Mrs Green and ten minutes after they had left David and Toby had finished the biscuits and the lemonade—which, as Toby said, was no good at all for squirting although they shook the bottles for *ages*. They would have played soldiers, but now that they had seen what a wonderful effect you can get with tomato ketchup and the tomato ketchup (or what was left of it) being locked in the house, the game didn't seem to them as exciting as it usually did.

On top of that the day was dull and cloudy. There was a sort of mistiness in the air and it wasn't particularly warm. It was, in fact, rapidly becoming a day-when-you-don't-know-what-to-do, and you know what *that's* like.

They wandered out of the garden gate into Parson's Lane and then they turned left and walked down the main road into the High Street of the village where they live, which is called Dingle Down. High Street was almost deserted because it was half-day closing and the only interesting thing that David and Toby came across was an empty cardboard shoe-box.

Now what makes an empty cardboard box interesting is the strange effect it has on boys and men—and even quite elderly and dignified gentlemen—when it's lying on the pavement. Hardly any of them can resist the temptation to give it a hefty kick in passing.

David and Toby, however, didn't kick it. They had a better idea. They picked it up carefully and hunted around until, just outside the shop-front of Mr Nuckle the butcher, which was being rebuilt, they found a large, red brick, and they put the brick in the middle of the pavement and put the cardboard box over it and hid round a corner to see what would happen.

They hadn't long to wait before Charlie Bogle, the biggest and toughest boy in Dingle Down, came slouching down the High Street.

When he was quite a way off he saw the box. He stopped and he looked. Then he tucked his elbows into his sides and began to trot towards the box. Then, as he got nearer, he broke into a run. He thundered down on the cardboard box and finally, with a loud cry of 'Goal!' he hit it, fairly and squarely, with a terrific kick.

'Ooh! Ow! My toe, my toe!' yelled Charlie Bogle, dancing around on one foot . . . and then he heard David and Toby laughing and he chased them all round Dingle Down for hours, it seemed, and they escaped him only by diving into a ditch, at the end of Farmer Gumbo's orchard, which had a fair amount of water in it but more mud.

When they felt they had really evaded Charlie Bogle they scrambled out of the ditch and they ran across two fields to get warm and finally found themselves slithering down a bank, right on to the platform of Dingle Down Halt railway station.

It was a lonely, deserted place. Some years ago the railway company had closed the station and taken away all the railway lines and some of the levers and things from the signal-box. But everything else they had left for the wind and the rain to demolish bit by bit. You'll have noticed that grown-ups object to children leaving their toys about, but they don't mind leaving things *they've* finished using—such as railway stations, pit-heaps, factories and even great gasworks—littered all over the place.

The light was beginning to fade and the empty railway station was a silent, eerie place. The mist began to thicken. It crept down from both ends of the platform. First it swirled around the station's big signboards that said DINGLE DOWN HALT, and they vanished. Then the goods office began to fade into the greyness, and then the great iron standard with the big electric bell that used to clang loudly when a train was due but was now silent and red-rusted all over. Soon David and Toby found themselves on a sort of island in the clammy cloud and the only things they could still see were the tiny waiting-room and the ticket office with its boarded-up window.

From the greyness above them black wires, that had long ago lost their electric bulbs, swung gently to and fro in the little eddies of mist, and the big black lampholders on the ends of them looked like great spiders.

'Ooh, I'm cold,' shivered David, clasping his hands together and blowing *hah* on them.

'I'm cold *and* hungry,' complained Toby, clasping his hands together and trying to warm them with a lot more *hah*. Then he shivered too, again and again, and he said, 'I don't call this fun.'

'Neither d-d-do I,' said David, his teeth beginning to chatter. 'I wish we were anywhere but here.'

And right at that moment . . . CLANG!!! the great bell on the platform sounded, making them almost jump out of their skins. CLANG . . . CLANG! it went. All the empty electric light sockets were suddenly filled with blazing lamps. Out of the curling white mist there came the wild shriek of a whistle, a sudden glare of red, and a strange clanking, growing louder and louder . . .

'It must be a train!' exclaimed Toby.

'But it can't be!' answered David, in a scared-y kind of voice.

'Well, what's that, then?' said Toby, pointing.

And he was right, for out of the mist there clattered into the station the strangest, oddest, most curious engine and train that the boys had ever seen.

The boiler of the locomotive seemed to be made of a

wooden barrel with shiny copper hoops around it. In front there was a high copper funnel, with the top splayed out like the mouth of a trumpet and belching smoke and red sparks. There was a tall whistle, worked by a string from the driver's platform, and a big copper dome, like a blister, on top of the boiler. Behind this there was a wooden cylinder, again bound with copper bands, which held the piston rod that turned the huge driving wheel. There was a very tiny tender, full of coal, and coupled to this was a little wooden van, marked GUARD.

And behind the guard's van—and this really made David and Toby rub their eyes—there was a landau, the kind of carriage that you see in royal processions being pulled by four horses and with coachmen sitting up in front. This carriage had had its wooden wheels taken off and its springs seemed to have been screwed down to a platform on which there were four iron wheels. The carriage, which was marked in big letters FIRST CLASS, had a striped canvas canopy slung high above it on iron posts.

David and Toby were taking all this in as the train clattered to a halt and the landau stopped right in front of them. The engine-driver and his fireman in their sooty dungarees scrambled down to the platform. Then the guard, in a dark blue uniform with red piping, got down and joined them. They all turned to face David and Toby and solemnly raised their caps. And then a very polite voice from behind the two boys murmured, 'Take your seats, gentlemen, please, All aboard for Mystery and Adventure! All aboard the Cobwebb Express!'

CHAPTER 2

LORD WRIGLEY COMES ABOARD

WELL, of course, as soon as they heard the name 'Cobwebb' both David and Toby knew exactly *what* had happened—although they couldn't for the moment think *why*. However, in case you haven't read about this mysterious person before, perhaps I'd better explain before we go any further.

You see, long ago, when the boys' Uncle Septimus Cobwebb was a boy himself, he went out into a meadow where fairies were supposed to dance and he left a note to his father saying he was going to sit in one of those dark green circles in the grass—the ones people call fairy rings—until the fairies appeared. Well, the fact is that Uncle Septimus Cobwebb never came home, not ever again. But one day Grandfather Cobwebb received a note from him in which he said he was well and happy but he was not coming back. He added that if any of the family needed help they should get in touch with him by a certain secret method.

Mr Green did this one day when David and Toby were bored and wanted an adventure, and in no time at all they found themselves in Septimus Cobwebb's crew of bold bluejackets fighting a horde of bloodthirsty pirates. Captain Cobwebb, as he now called himself, was so pleased with their bravery that he gave them a kind of private radio link directly with him—to use whenever they wanted another adventure.*

'Why, *that's* it!' exclaimed David. 'Remember, Toby, when Uncle Septimus made that little blue mark come at the bottom of the first finger of our right hands, and then he said if we touch it with the little finger of the left hand and spoke a message, it would go straight to him? Well, one of us must have done it accidentally when we were rubbing our hands together to try to get them warm . . .'

'Yes,' cried Toby, 'and you remember you said, "I wish we were anywhere but here." Uncle Septimus must have heard us, and . . . and . . .'

'Precisely, gentlemen!' said the polite voice behind them and they swung round to see the Station Master beaming at them. He was a large, round man, with a large, round, red face and he had long, pointed white whiskers that came down from his ears almost to his waist. His smart blue uniform and pill-box hat were a blaze of gold lace and in his left hand he held a huge gold watch that

* See *Captain Cobwebb*

was ticking away as loudly as a grandfather clock. 'Precisely, gentlemen,' he repeated. 'An adventure is about to begin. But first, Captain Cobwebb wishes me to remind you of the regulations before you embark. Do you promise that once the adventure has started you will never give in nor turn back, but see it right through to the end, whatever the dangers?'

'We promise,' said David and Toby together.

'Then kindly take your seats,' replied the Station Master, moving forward and opening the door of the landau with a deep bow and a flourish. The engine-driver and fireman climbed on to the footplate and the fireman began to shovel coal into the glowing firebox while the driver stood with one hand on the great starting-lever and the other on the cord that worked the whistle.

And, as David and Toby sank back luxuriously among the velvet cushions, a shrill alarm bell sounded from the Station Master's huge watch, the whistle shrieked, the guard waved his green flag as he swung on to the step of his van, flames and sparks shot from the high funnel, the engine went CHUGG . . . CHUGG . . . chugg-chugg-chugg-chugg-chugg . . . the couplings drew taut with a clank and a jerk and . . .

And above all the screeching and the hiss of steam, the boys suddenly heard a voice crying, 'Ho, ho, ho! A moment, please! A little moment!' and there appeared out of the mist at the far end of the platform a boyish figure about Toby's height—a dark-skinned youngster in a close-fitting, high-necked jacket and long, tight, white trousers, with a kind of large wickerwork vase clutched under one arm.

The figure simply flew along on twinkling, sandalled feet. It ducked under the Station Master's arm as he began to close the door of the landau and leaped into the carriage.

'Good evening! . . . Good evening!' the boy greeted David and Toby breathlessly. 'I beg of you, entreat this most noble official to restrain this impatient vehicle, if only for a moment. Lord Wrigley is coming . . . he is coming . . . he will be here in seconds . . .'

'I'm sorry, sir,' said the Station Master. 'But I've no authority . . .'

'He comes . . . he comes,' begged the stranger. 'I could not run fast enough to catch the train if I carried him. So I put him down and came ahead to entreat you to wait for him. You see, he cannot move as speedily as I. He has no legs . . .'

'No legs?' said David and Toby together, astounded.

'No legs?' echoed the Station Master. 'Then how's he going to get here? I'm afraid I can't hold up the train any longer, not even for a lord. Look at the time!' And he tapped his great gold watch impatiently.

'Just a moment, revered sir . . . a little moment!' pleaded the boy. 'I will try to speed Lord Wrigley on his way.' And suddenly there appeared between his hands a strange instrument like a small wooden trumpet with a great blob between the mouthpiece and the horn end. He placed the instrument to his lips and began to play an eerie melody of high and whining notes.

'Oh! Oh! Oh!' yelled the Station Master, dashing into the ticket office and slamming the door.

'He comes!' cried the boy. 'Come, Lord Wrigley . . . faster, O noble lord . . . the train is ready to go . . .'

'Oh!' gasped David and 'Oh!' gasped Toby, both shrinking into the corners of the seat.

'Come, Lord Wrigley,' called the boy joyfully. 'Your carriage awaits. Your basket is warm and cosy. You shall eat and sleep after your great race. Welcome, O wisest and most speedy of all the Nagas!'

And as the boy said this, there slid into the carriage an absolutely enormous snake. Its forked tongue flickered in and out and, as its eyes turned towards them, David and Toby saw the black, spectacle-like markings on its head which showed that this was none other than . . . *a deadly cobra.* At this moment came a final shriek from the whistle and a great heave from the engine. All the lights on the station platform suddenly went out and David and Toby found themselves moving faster and faster through the black, black night . . . alone in the darkness with the unknown passenger and his fearsome companion.

CHAPTER 3

WHAT'S IN A HISS?

DAVID and Toby were thoroughly scared—and they were even more scared when a perfect gale of hissing broke out in the darkness from the seat opposite.

'Oh, David,' whispered Toby, 'd-d-d'you think it's going to attack us?'

'I h-hope not,' answered David, 'but keep your voice down—it might not like being called just "it" instead of "lord".'

The hissing went on and on and it seemed, thought David, to have a kind of pattern in it, because certain kinds of hisses were being repeated. Indeed it sounded as if the boy and his cobra companion were having some sort of argument.

And then a very remarkable idea began to come into David's mind as he listened more closely to the hissing, which was a mixture of little hisses and long drawn-out hisses and went like this:

the strange boy: 'Ss-ss-ss . . . ss-ssss-ss-ss . . . ss . . . ss . . .
ss-ssss-ssss-ss . . . ss-ssss-ss-ss . . .
ssss-ssss-ssss . . .
ss-ssss-ss . . . ssss-ss-ss.'

the cobra: 'Ssss-ss . . . ssss-ssss-ssss . . .
ssss-ss . . . ssss-ssss-ssss . . . ssss
. . . ssss-ss-ssss-ssss . . . ss . . . ssss.'

And David listened, and he listened, and suddenly he whispered to Toby, 'The boy said "Sleep, lord" and Lord Wrigley said "No! Not yet." ' Toby said, 'But how do you know?' And David whispered, 'Because they're talkin Morse Code. Shut up! I'm listening.'

Of course as soon as Toby had the clue all the Morse

Code lessons they had had at the Wolf Club meetings came back to him and he found he could understand, too. If you write down every *ssss* as a dash and every *ss* as a dot, you'll see that David was quite correct.

Well, the hissing argument went on and on until suddenly both the boy and the cobra seemed to run out of breath. And in that pause David began to hiss himself.

Now I don't suppose for a moment that the printer has enough *ssss's* to print a whole conversation in snake-talk, and besides it would take up an awful amount of space, so we'll just have to remember that any talking with Lord Wrigley *is* in Morse. David began rather slowly,

---

TEACH YOURSELF SNAKE-TALK

Just in case you should ever meet a cobra, or indeed, any snake that happens to be in a talkative mood, prepare yourself now so that you can take part in an intelligent conversation with it.

You won't go amiss if you hiss like this:

ssss—long hiss   ss—short hiss

The Vowels

A ss-ssss   E ss   I ss-ss
O ssss-ssss-ssss   U ss-ss-ssss

The Consonants

B ssss-ss-ss-ss   C ssss-ss-ssss-ss
D ssss-ss-ss   F ss-ss-ssss-ss
G ssss-ssss-ss   H ss-ss-ss-ss
J ss-ssss-ssss-ssss   K ssss-ss-ssss
L ss-ssss-ss-ss   M ssss-ssss
N ssss-ss   P ss-ssss-ssss-ss
Q ssss-ssss-ss-ssss   R ss-ssss-ss
S ss-ss-ss   T ssss
V ss-ss-ss-ssss   W ss-ssss-ssss
X ssss-ss-ss-ssss   Y ssss-ss-ssss-ssss
Z ssss-ssss-ss-ss

The Numbers

1 ss-ssss-ssss-ssss-ssss   2 ss-ss-ssss-ssss-ssss
3 ss--ss-ss-ssss-ssss   4 ss-ss-ss-ss-ssss
5 ss-ss-sss-ss-ss   6 ssss-ss-ss-ss-ss
7 ssss-ssss-ss-ss-ss   8 ssss-ssss-ssss-ss-ss
9 ssss-ssss-ssss-ssss-ss   10 ssss-ssss-ssss-ssss-ssss

Note: Boa-constrictors don't hiss. They will talk to you by means of long and short squeezes. It isn't always easy to answer a boa-constrictor, however.

---

because he wasn't very experienced, and what he hissed was, 'O noble lord, my brother and I humbly greet you.'

As soon as David had done this, the strange boy cried out in delight but the cobra immediately hissed at him, 'You be quiet! Hold your tongue! Speak when you are spoken to! . . . I am glad,' the cobra said to David, 'to note that you address me with the respect that is my due. I shall be graciously pleased to learn your names.'

So David told him and the cobra said, 'Ah yes, interesting. I must remember them. *How* shall I remember them?' he asked, hissing slowly to himself as if he were suddenly becoming very tired. 'I shall remember the name David because it was a David who killed a giant called Goliath. And I shall remember Toby . . . because . . .' and the hisses became slower and slower and softer and softer '. . . I shall remember Toby because . . . yes, because of what Hamlet said: "Toby or not Toby? That is the question." Now I shall sssssleep,' hissed Lord Wrigley and they heard his basket creak as he settled himself comfortably and then, after a most unlordly snore, there was silence.

From the darkness the strange boy spoke—but not in the hissing code, for which David and Toby were glad, because it makes conversation rather a slow business.

'My name is Arif,' he said. 'Now my lord is sleeping, we can talk. Do you wish for light?'

'Oh yes,' said David, and Toby asked, 'Where's the switch?'

'There is none,' replied Arif. 'We will make our own light. Wait but a moment.'

So they sat waiting and in a few seconds the boys saw a tiny white light, which slowly grew in size. Soon they could see that it was floating between the palms of Arif's hands, which he moved round and round as you do when you are rolling a piece of clay into a ball.

Faster and faster moved his hands and the globe of light grew in size and brightness until it was as big as a cricket ball, and they could see each other and Arif and the wicker basket in which Lord Wrigley slept as clearly as if the sun were shining.

Suddenly Arif released the light and it floated slowly upwards until it came to rest against the canvas canopy above them. And there it stayed, filling the carriage with a warm glow as they sped through the darkness.

'Arif!' exclaimed David. 'How on earth did you do that?'

'It is but a little magic that I was taught by my lord,' said the boy. 'But speak softly . . . I would not have him wakened.'

'You mean *snakes* know magic?' demanded Toby.

'You mean your snake *taught* you?' began David in amazement.

'Sssh!' replied Arif. 'It would offend him mightily to hear you call him *my* snake. He is my *guru*—that means my teacher—and I am his pupil and his servant.'

'Is that why you call him "my lord"?' asked Toby.

'It is,' answered Arif, 'for in my country, India, we know that the Nagas—that means snakes—are really powerful gods. Indeed the fifth day of the month of Shravam, which begins in your month of July, is dedicated to them. This one, my teacher, instructs me in many mysteries and in return I serve him and I play to him on the pipe, for he loves to sway to its movements.'

Toby, however, still had a question and the same one was on David's lips. But Toby got in first. 'Why do you call him Wrigley?' he asked.

'It was his wish,' answered Arif surprisingly. 'One day, when he was swaying to my pipe in front of a large and admiring crowd, a little girl addressed him by that name. As soon as she saw him she clapped her hands in delight and cried, "Oh! Wonderful wriggly wriggly!" My lord was entranced. He told me that the name she called him had the most snakely and moving sound he had ever heard in his life and that from then on he would take it for his own.'

'Well, it was a pretty good choice,' said David with a chuckle, but all Toby said was, 'I'm *famished!* I'm dying for something to eat!' Toby soon loses interest in any subject at all when he begins to feel hungry.

'Famished? No need to be famished,' said a strange

The guard on the mysterious train uncouples the carriage in which David and Toby and their strange companions are travelling . . and off it goes, careering downhill all on its own in the darkness. It was while they were being buffeted about that Toby discovered the buffet.

voice and they all looked up to see the head of the guard sticking out of the window at the back of his cabin.

'Plenty of food in the compartment,' said the guard. 'Lift the seats. Sandwiches there. Cakes. Ice-cream. Fizzy drinks. No need to go hungry, sir. Slipping your compartment here. Have a good trip.' And with that, the guard gripped a large iron lever over the top of the window and pulled it smartly down.

'What's he mean about slipping our compartment?' said Toby irritably.

'*That's* what he means!' said David. 'Look, Toby! Arif—look!'

For suddenly the carriage was swinging away to the right while the engine, sparks belching from its funnel, was rapidly dwindling away with its guard's van into the darkness.

'He's undone the couplings!' cried David. 'The engine's left us. We're on our own and we're going downhill!' He was right about that for the carriage was beginning to pick up speed rapidly and it was swaying from side to side. 'What are we going to do now?' he demanded.

Arif said nothing but made a dive to grab Lord Wrigley's basket before it was hurled to the floor. Then Toby answered. He had lifted up one of the seats and had been grubbing about in the box-like compartment underneath. 'I know what *I'm* going to do,' he said. 'I'm going to eat a *hundred* sausage-rolls. There are *millions* in here!'

CHAPTER 4

SECRET ORDERS!

OF course, Toby was exaggerating a bit in his excitement, but who wouldn't be excited if he'd been getting hungrier and hungrier and suddenly discovered he'd been sitting over a whole great collection of food?

Food of all kinds there was, not only sausage-rolls

(which are among Toby's favourite snacks), but strawberry jam tarts, meat pies, sponge cake with butter-icing an inch and a half thick in the middle, five different flavours of potato crisps, cream puffs, prawn crackers, banana custard, peanut butter and absolutely *dozens* of different kinds of sandwiches—white bread, brown bread, sticky bread and currant bread—together with bottles and bottles of Cherry Sparkle and Ice-Cream Soda . . . as much as anybody could possibly drink, with plenty of spare bottles left over for squirting at people.

David went across the carriage and squeezed on the seat with Arif, so that the basket in which Lord Wrigley was sleeping was held safely upright between them. Toby, meanwhile, squatted down in the box-like seat and, firmly wedged, began handing out food to David and Arif while he kept up a running commentary on what he was eating himself.

If Mrs Green had heard him, she would have said, 'Don't speak with your mouth full, Toby!' but she wasn't there and anyway both David and Arif were too busy eating to listen to him, which was just as well because they would have found some difficulty in understanding things like this: *'Shay, David! You should try shoshidge-roll with banana cushtard. Itsh shmashing!'* Or *'Put shome prawn crackersh on a shtrawberry tart.'* Or 'Try *dunking eggan-cresh shanwichesh in Ishe-Cream Shoda.'* It didn't matter, anyway, that the others weren't listening to him, because Toby didn't expect an answer and if he'd got one he couldn't have heard it because his jaws were champing away so noisily.

It was only after quite a time, when the three boys had got past the gobbling stage and the hearty-eating stage and the slow-eating stage and had reached the nibble-(heavy breathing)-another-nibble stage that any notice was taken of a remark by Toby.

He had sampled pretty nearly everything there was under the seat and he was feeling around in the corners to find out if there was anything that he hadn't yet tasted. Suddenly he said disgustedly, 'Ugh! Who on earth wants an *ostrich* egg?'

And straight away up went the lid of Lord Wrigley's basket and out popped the head of the cobra himself, swaying from side to side, with his long forked tongue flicking rapidly in and out.

'An egg?' he hissed excitedly. 'An egg? Wonderful. Give it to me, boy. Quickly! Quickly!'

Toby stretched out his hand, then pulled it back.

'Oh, I'm sorry. Lord Wrigley,' he said, 'I think it's hard-boiled. Shouldn't I take the shell off for you?'

At this the cobra almost exploded in a torrent of hisses.

'The shell off!' he babbled (and if you don't believe that it's possible to babble in Morse Code, just ask any ship's radio officer). 'The shell off, indeed! That's the best part. GIVE ME THAT EGG!'

Toby, thoroughly scared, reached out his hand and Lord Wrigley opened his mouth wide . . . and wider . . . and still wider, until Toby thought it would split right round and his head fall off. But slowly, slowly, the great egg began to slip down the cobra's throat. Then it showed as an enormous bulge behind his head and, very gradually, it began to move down, and down . . . and down. And then it reached the neck of the basket. *And there it stuck.*

Both David and Toby—and even Arif, to judge by his expression—expected an angry outburst from the snake, but Lord Wrigley just moved his head from side to side in a very satisfied way and wiggled his tongue about as though he was licking his lips.

'Most satisfying . . . most delectable,' hissed Lord Wrigley. 'Most comfortable and relaxed position. Most exhilarating ride. Arif, while this meal is digesting, to your lessons, boy! First, the Stretching Spell. Raise the right arm . . . now the Spell . . .'

And Arif, his right arm held out level with his shoulder, began to whisper,

Lengthen, humerus,
One and twomerus.
Ulna, radius,
Don't be afraidius.

And as Toby and David watched in amazement, they saw Arif's arm growing longer and longer until it reached right across the carriage, past Toby's head, over the back of the carriage and two feet out into space!

'How many times have you practised this?' asked the cobra.

'One thousand eight hundred times, my lord,' answered Arif.

'Yes . . . yes . . . Well, not bad—for a beginner,' hissed Lord Wrigley. He sounded rather like a school-teacher, Toby thought. 'Yes, well, that will do.' And back went Arif's arm, in a twinkling, to its normal size.

'Most excellent meal,' said Lord Wrigley softly and in a rather tired manner. 'Do need a nap. But just one more exercise. I think you have rather a gift for Head Vanishing. You generally vanish your own quite effectively, Arif. Now see if you can vanish it and those of your two young friends as well.'

'Here, I say . . . !' began David and 'W-w-w-what-t . . . ?' began Toby. But Arif said quickly, 'Be not afraid. You are my friends. And it is but an illusion.'

'Do it any time,' hissed Lord Wrigley. 'Perfectly simple. Watch . . .' And suddenly his head just vanished into thin air and there was nothing to see but his neck (or his body: how do you tell which is which on a snake?) and the egg he had eaten, still resting on the neck of the wicker basket. 'And here we are again!' remarked the cobra, his head appearing as suddenly as it had vanished. 'Proceed, Arif.'

Arif began to wave his hands in a curious manner and then, *phut*, there was no head on his shoulders at all. And then: 'Toby, you haven't got a head!' cried David. 'David, your head's vanished!' cried Toby. Then *phut* . . . all three heads were back again.

'See?' hissed Lord Wrigley. And at that moment the egg he had been digesting slipped through the neck of the basket. Down went the cobra's head, down fell the lid of the basket and from inside there came the gentle, regular sort of *zizzing*. His lordship was asleep.

'Will you teach us to do magic like that, Arif?' asked David.

'If my lord agrees,' smiled Arif, 'and if you are prepared to practise every day for ten or twelve years . . .

But there is perhaps some lesser magic I can teach you.' Then he stopped suddenly. 'But what is it, Toby?' he asked. 'What have you found?' For Toby, who had clambered out of the box-seat was standing, looking very puzzled, with a large white envelope in his hand.

'I just found this in there,' he said, 'and look what it says on the front.' He held out the envelope to David and Arif. On it, in bold black letters, was printed:

SECRET ORDERS

To be opened immediately.

'Well go on, then, open it, chump!' cried David, and Toby tore open the envelope and drew out a small sheet of paper, and he read this message:

To David, Toby and their companion Arif:
Find the King and restore him to his throne.
Signed *Uncle Septimus*
(CAPTAIN COBWEBB)

CHAPTER 5

PRECIPICE AHEAD!

'FIND the King and restore him to his throne!' repeated David. 'But what king?'

'And how shall we recognise him?' demanded Toby.

'And I have a question too, David,' said Arif. 'Who is this Captain Cobwebb?'

Well, of course David and Toby could answer that question and they galloped through the whole history of their Uncle Septimus until David suddenly said, 'Ssh! If we wake Lord Wrigley he might be annoyed.'

'We had better speak softly,' agreed Arif, 'but there is no need to whisper. All snakes, you know, are rather deaf because the bones inside their ears are connected up the wrong way. That is why you must always hiss very distinctly when you speak to my lord. And that is why, also, I use this pipe, which makes a very penetrating sound, when I call him from a distance or play to him.'

'Poor Lord Wrigley,' said Toby. 'Is he very old then?'

At that there was a sharp rustle from the basket, the lid lifted slightly and the cobra's head popped out through the opening.

'Where *do* you get these silly ideas from?' he hissed angrily. 'Old? I'm not a day over seven hundred years . . .'

'The prime of life, mighty lord,' said David quickly.

'Exactly,' answered Lord Wrigley, forgetting his anger at once. 'Old in experience but young in outlook. You are most perspicacious, young Goliath . . .'

'*David*, my lord,' Arif corrected. '*David* is our companion's name.'

'Eh? Oh yes,' hissed the cobra. 'He's the one who threw the stone at the giant. Yes. Brave boy. Good shooting. Going back to sleep now. Don't let me hear any more nonsensical remarks . . .' And Lord Wrigley's head began to slide back under the lid.

'Please, my lord,' begged Arif. 'Tell me, did you know of this Septimus Cobwebb and his orders and is it because of them that you brought me here?'

Lord Wrigley poked his head out again. 'Yes, yes and yes,' he hissed. 'You worked hard at your lessons. I thought you needed a change. Then Cobwebb suggested I should let you join in this adventure. Good idea, I thought. Might give you a chance to try out a bit of magic. So I said we'd come . . .'

'And do you *really* know our Uncle Septimus?' asked Toby, excited.

'Know him?' hissed Lord Wrigley. 'I should say I do! Known him for years. Member of my club in Calcutta—the Cobra Club. Oh yes. And I heard a lot from him about you, Goliath and you, Hamlet . . .'

'Not Goliath, my lord,' Arif reminded him. 'Not Goliath but *David*. Not Hamlet, but *Toby*.'

'Of course, of course,' agreed the cobra sleepily, as his head began to slip back under the lid. 'Knew it was something out of Shakespeare. But not Hamlet, eh? Must be . . .' and Lord Wrigley's hissing grew slower and slower and softer and softer, 'must be . . . in some other play, then.' And he vanished into his basket.

The three boys went back to their discussion about Captain Cobwebb's orders.

'This journey must end somewhere,' said Arif. 'And then we must ask what country we are in and if the king is missing.'

'But suppose it's a country like America,' objected Toby, 'where they don't have a king anyway?'

'Then we'll just have to find our way to a country where they have a king but he's got lost,' answered David, '—or he's been kidnapped or something.'

'But that might take ages and ages!' said Toby, and the thought made him feel so hungry that he grabbed a sausage-roll in each hand and began munching furiously.

'Yes,' said Arif, thoughtfully. 'Toby is wise. If we are to travel far in strange lands, how shall we live? We must earn our bread. I can play upon my pipe and my lord will rise from his basket and sway this way and that before the people. And they will marvel at him and say, "Behold the boy plays music and the snake dances to it." And they will give us, we hope, a little money. But there are three of us to feed, besides my lord. I know you have no magic, David, nor you, Toby, and it would take a long time to teach you some. Is there anything you can do that would entertain the people?'

'I can do handsprings,' said David.

'And I can juggle a bit,' said Toby. 'I can keep three tennis balls in the air at once. But we haven't any tennis balls.'

'There are very few places in the world where you cannot pick up three stones,' laughed Arif, and Toby said he thought they would be just as good.

'Anything else?' asked Arif.

'Well,' said David doubtfully, 'Toby and I have been having some judo lessons. Perhaps we could put on a show. Toby could pretend to be a robber and attack me and I could throw him over my shoulder . . .'

'Or you could attack me and I could throw *you* over *my* shoulder,' put in Toby, hastily, and it looked as if one of these 'I'll be leader—No, *I'll* be leader' arguments was going to break out when Arif said, 'Why not take turns?' and that settled the matter. David and Toby began to discuss the things they would do when Arif said, 'It grows light . . . and look . . . *look*!'

For the blackness had suddenly given way to greyness, the greyness to a thin white mist, the mist to patches of blue sky, to glimpses of grass and shrubs around them, and . . . '*Look!*' cried Arif again, kneeling on the seat and pointing ahead and downwards.

And then they saw their peril!

The carriage was hurtling towards the lip of a great basin of mountains. Far, far below, in the bottom of the basin, they could see a round hill, covered with buildings and topped by a castle, and around the bottom of this hill was a great wall with towers and battlements. To the right and left of the carriage the boys could see where the mountain ridge they were on fell away to the plain. And they knew that in a matter of moments, the carriage, swaying dizzily at high speed, would shoot over the edge of the precipice. There was nothing to do but . . .

'Hold tight!' yelled David.

And with that the carriage ran *crash!* into a huge boulder. There was a rending of wood and metal, the bolts that fixed it to the trolley below sheared off, and the carriage, with nothing now beneath it but its curved springs, shot over the edge of the precipice and began to plummet like a stone to the plain beneath!

CHAPTER 6

THE LAW OF THE TWEDS

THE three boys clung to the stanchions that supported the canopy as the carriage plunged down and the air screamed past them. The canopy caught the blast and stretched and billowed out like a parachute. They felt the speed of the descent being checked . . . but slowly, very slowly.

They could see the cliff racing upwards. Below, details of the countryside became bigger and clearer, like pictures seen through a zoom lens . . . winding white roads, green pastures, streams, great groups of trees. The wall around the city was terribly high and thick, with no way into the city behind it except for one huge gateway, whose vast double doors, strengthened with great iron bands, seemed firmly shut.

Then David shouted, 'Hold tight! The canopy's tearing away!'

And as he spoke, with a ripping and rending of fabric, the canopy was torn from its moorings and swept up into the mist with Arif's magic ball of light still glowing through its folds.

The fabric, however, had held together long enough to keep the carriage on an even keel as it hit the earth, fair and square, the supple springs underneath took the strain and then . . . *whoops* . . . the carriage shot into the air once more and bounced towards the frowning walls of the city in a series of great hops . . . nearer and nearer, until they could see every detail of the battlements, every iron stud in the enormous door.

'We're going to hit the wall!' shouted Toby and then they all held their breath. But, with the last leap of all, the carriage just cleared the top of the gateway and landed softly and without overturning in a clump of bushes part way up the grassy slope of the hill on which stood the strange city.

'Phew,' whistled David as the carriage quivered to rest. Toby grabbed a meat pie to help him recover.

'Arif,' said David, 'is Lord Wrigley all right?'

'Mercifully, he sleeps,' replied Arif, after a quick peep into the basket. 'After such a meal as he had, my lord's slumbers may last for many hours. Let us also rest a while, then we must find the name of this city.'

'That won't be difficult,' David said. 'Just look over there!'

For only a short distance away there stood a huge white

notice-board and the words upon it were in such big, bold black letters that the boys could read them easily from where they sat. This is what the notice said:

WELCOME to MUDL
CAPITAL OF URRAYRIA

KEEP OUT!
ADMISSION FREE
PAY at the GATE

URRAYRIA GREETS YOU!
VISITORS WILL BE SHOT

'Well, what do you make of that?' demanded David.

'I am bewildered,' confessed Arif.

'Well, you won't be bewildered for long,' said Toby. 'There's a whole lot of people coming down the road.' And out of the city above ran a crowd of men and women, shouting and gesticulating. At their head were two men, each trying to get ahead of the other. One of them, who seemed to be making the pace, carried a large basket. The other, a huge burly fellow, grasped in both hands a great oaken bar with a chain on the end, to which was fastened a huge ball of iron with long spikes sticking out all around it. He kept pausing at intervals to whirl this ugly weapon round his head and then he would go pounding along to try to overtake the man with the basket.

'I don't like the look of this,' said David. 'Shall we run for it?'

'Where can we run?' said Arif. 'There is no way of escape.'

'What shall we do, then?' demanded David, who doesn't like to take things lying down.

Then Toby spoke. 'Have a shandwich,' he said (with his mouth full, I'm afraid)). 'Itsh breakfash-time anyway. Can't deshide anything on an empty shtomach.'

David saw the wisdom of this and Arif suggested that it might also be a good idea to stuff as much food as they could into their pockets. 'Because,' he said, 'if these very curious folk do not kill us they may throw us into prison or turn us out of the city. And we may have to travel far before we find a friendly village. But now let us eat and greet them courteously and without showing any fear.'

And so it was that when the throng of townsfolk came up to the carriage, they found the three boys calmly munching away and swigging long cool draughts of Cherry Sparkle like any normal group of picnickers. The crowd wavered and came to a halt, shuffling their feet, whispering and ill at ease. Of the two leaders it was the man with the basket who reached the carriage first. He bowed low and then held out the basket towards them.

'Welcome, strangers, to Mudl, capital of the happy land of Urrayria,' he said, smiling. 'Accept this bread and this milk, traditional gifts of greeting to all who come in peace.' But as David took the basket into the carriage and was about to reply to the greeting, the swarthy, beetle-browed man shouldered the other to one side and, holding high his iron skull-cracker, he cried, 'Kill these people! The law says kill them!' And he jerked his head towards the great notice-board.

'No,' replied the other. 'The law says we should welcome our visitors. Would you defy the ruling of the Tweds?'

All the crowd fell silent and the beetle-browed man looked very uncomfortable. Then he said, 'How new is this law?'

'It is the newest of all laws," said the other, 'and therefore the one to be obeyed. It was passed by the Council cf the Tweds at three candles after the noon of yesterday.'

'Ha!' cried the beetle-browed man triumphantly, 'but the law of death was passed by the Council at *five* candles after noon. This then, is the law in force and these strangers must die,' and he turned on the boys. 'How did you get here?' he demanded. 'And why did you come?'

Toby began, 'Well now, you see, it was like this . . .' when David kicked him on the ankle and whispered, 'Shut up. They'll never believe all *that* story.' And he stood up and bowed to the man and said, 'We were out riding and we just dropped in to see your beautiful city' (which was certainly the truth).

'Our beautiful city!' exclaimed the people in the crowd. 'You see, Mudl is famous! They came to see our beautiful city. Surely this is no killing matter?'

'Silence!' roared Beetle-brows. 'They must die. I shall carry out the law of the Tweds. Shall I tell the Great Council that you wished to defy their order?' And he braced himself, feet apart, and prepared to deal the first death blow.

It seemed to David and Toby and Arif that the whole adventure was coming to a sudden and terrible end. But at that moment a loud voice cried, 'Stop! If you kill them you will condemn yourself to death!'

It was the voice of the man with the basket. The other dropped his arms, and before he could speak the man with the basket went on, 'You say you are carrying out the law of death. But look at the notice. The law does not say that visitors shall be clubbed to death. It says they shall be shot.'

'Shooting or clubbing,' growled Beetle-brows, 'it's all the same. They die, don't they?'

The other answered patiently, 'The law of the Tweds says "shoot" and shooting calls for crossbows. To preserve the peace of this realm all crossbows are kept in the armoury of the castle and only the Tweds can give permission for their use. So you see, my foolish fellow, that we must take these visitors before the Council of the Tweds, because it is the Tweds alone who can rule whether they are to be slain.'

'Then *you* can bring them along,' growled Beetle-brows. 'I shall go ahead and warn our masters that you will follow with these spies.' And he shouldered his way through the crowd and made off up the hill.

'That was a close shave!' David whispered to Arif.

'Yes,' Arif answered. 'This man has proved himself a friend in need.'

'Jolly glad he's on our side,' added Toby, as the man with the basket opened the carriage door and smilingly helped them down. He led them up the hill, the chattering townspeople straggling behind. Then David nudged Arif and Arif turned to the man and he said, 'Noble sir, my companions and I wish to offer to you our most heartfelt gratitude for saving us from that man.'

'Oh, but please,' said the man, smiling with pleasure, 'there is no need to thank me. I was only trying to ensure that the law was properly observed. In my opinion,' he added cheerfully, 'you will all undoubtedly be shot. But you will have the great pleasure of knowing that the shooting is perfectly, perfectly legal.'

CHAPTER 7

IN THE CHAMBER OF DOOM

'BUT it's not fair!' exploded David. 'I mean, you put all those things on the notice-board—*Welcome to Urrayria* mixed up with *Visitors will be shot*. If it had just said we'd be shot we'd have gone away at once. Why,' David added, 'even *you* didn't know what the law was! Why don't you rub out the old laws and leave only the latest one on the notice-board?'

'Oh, come now,' smiled the Basket-man, 'think of the expense! What's the use of rubbing something out when you'll almost certainly have to paint it in again next day? You see,' he went on, 'in order to be absolutely fair to everybody the Great Council of Tweds examine the country's laws *every day*—and they generally change 'em right round the other way. Couldn't be fairer than that, could you?

'I mean, take your case. Now we've been having trouble with the Nings—they want something we have and they've been sending spies into the city to find out where it's hidden. Obviously we can't keep on welcoming such visitors with gifts! I mean it would be silly, wouldn't it?

'So we decide to shoot visitors, to be on the safe side. Then you come along, sightseeing, and this morning we shoot you. Now this afternoon, when the Tweds reconsider the laws, the Great Council may feel that we've shot innocent visitors, they'll change the law back again from shooting to welcoming . . .'

'And a fat lot of good that'll do us!' exclaimed David.

'In my humble opinion this is ree-diculous,' said Arif.

And Toby, who was carrying the welcome-basket and had now started nibbling on a crusty loaf said, 'Itsh abshlootly shilly.'

'You are wrong,' said the Basket-man calmly, 'and I will prove it. First, do you agree that one should always look at both sides of a question?'

Of course, the boys had to say yes to this and the Basket-man went on, 'And you do agree, don't you, with the old saying that two heads are better than one?' Naturally, they said that they did (after all, that's what grown-ups were always telling them).

'Then you have just agreed,' said the Basket-man triumphantly, 'that Urrayria has the perfect government—because every member of the Great Council of the Tweds possesses two heads (that, of course, is why they are called Tweds) and, as you agreed, two heads are better than one. The next thing is that each member of the Great Council looks at both sides of a question. He *has* to, because each of his heads thinks entirely the opposite of the other one.'

There was a long silence, while the three boys were considering this fantastic piece of information.

Toby was the first to speak. Hastily swallowing the last mouthful of bread, he said, 'But . . . but . . . if a Twed has two heads, does that mean he can eat two dinners at once?'

'Oh no,' laughed the man, 'he doesn't have two heads on his shoulders at the same time . . .'

'Well, what's he do with the one he isn't . . . isn't . . . I mean, the one he isn't wearing?' asked David.

'Inside the council chamber,' said the Basket-man, 'he would put it on the council table, in front of him. In the street, of course, he'd probably carry it under his arm, to keep its ears warm.'

'I think, sir,' put in Arif, gently, 'that what we all really wish to know is: how do these gentlemen *use* these two heads when they are in the Great Council of the Tweds?'

'It works like this,' said the Basket-man. 'This morning the Great Council meet and each member will wear the head that he had on when he passed yesterday's laws. The council will pass sentences for any offences committed under those laws—they'll shoot you, for instance,' he added. 'When they've finished this business, each member will remove his head and replace it with the other head which sees every question from the opposite point of view. All the laws will then be reconsidered and, as a general rule, changed round completely. It could be that tomorrow we should be ordered to welcome you to Mudl instead of shooting you.'

'It'll be a bit late for welcomes by that time!' snorted Toby, and they shuffled along, weary, silent and very glum. The Basket-man, who seemed to feel that everybody should be happy about his explanation, began to whistle cheerfully and there was a constant buzz of chatter from the townspeople following them to the great turreted building in which their fate would soon be decided.

Just at this moment there came a soft, insistent hissing from the depths of Lord Wrigley's basket. Arif nudged David and David dug Toby in the ribs and they listened very very hard. The great cobra was hissing out instructions. This took some time and they were almost at the door of the council building before he had finished his message.

What Lord Wrigley told them was this: 'Remember what the man told you: The Tweds first pass sentence and after that they change the laws. You must find a way of taking their minds off this business of shooting you. Keep them thinking about something else until it is time for them to reconsider yesterday's laws. Once they have changed the law to welcoming visitors instead of shooting them you will be safe—and then we can get away from this place before they change their minds again.'

'But, my lord,' whispered Arif. 'How shall we do this thing? How make them forget the shooting?'

'Use your head, boy,' replied the cobra. 'Surely, if two

heads are better than one, then three heads are better than two?'

'But suppose after all that they leave the law as it is and still decide to shoot us?' demanded David.

'Let's not be gloomy,' hissed Lord Wrigley. 'If it *does* come to that, then we'll all *four* get our heads together. That should make us twice as smart as any Twed. And now tell young Hamlet—sorry, young Toby—to push one of those bottles of milk into my basket. Thanks,' said Lord Wrigley. 'A pint of milk and a nice snooze and I'll be ready for anything.'

They had now passed under the frowning archway, had crossed a dark hall and stood before a big oaken door on which the Basket-man knocked. The door creaked ajar and a helmeted head was poked out.

'The visitors,' said the Basket-man, pushing the boys forward. 'These are the visitors . . . you know, they have to be shot under the new Law Seven.'

'About time they got here, too!' snorted the soldier. 'Everybody's been dealt with except this lot. Coming late to the Great Council indeed! Another five minutes and they'd have decided to flog you as well as shoot you, I shouldn't wonder. Come on in,' he said roughly, and as the boys filed through the narrow opening, he pushed the Basket-man back into the crowd and slammed the door on the lot of them.

Inside the hall it was darker still and, as the soldier pricked them forward with the tip of his spear, all that the boys could see in front of them was the vague outline of some wooden steps. A great noise of shouting and roaring was going on and there was a frenzied clatter of steel-shod feet on a stone floor.

'Get up the steps into the box,' growled the soldier, jabbing at them mercilessly. 'Face the Great Council, bow to Hedtwed and to the Tweds assembled. And for goodness' sake,' he grated, 'do your best not to breathe. There's only one candle left and if that's blown out then we'll *all* be shot.'

Up the steps they stumbled, into the cramped oaken dock. And, as they eyes at last pierced the gloom, they found themselves face to face with the Great Council of Urrayia—the terrible Tweds.

CHAPTER 8

THE MYSTERIOUS PRISONER

OVER the heads of court ushers and soldiers, who were dashing here and there across the wide flagged floor of the council chamber, they could just make out, in the flickering light of a solitary candle, the shapes of five figures seated at a high table.

The candle, which had burned down to its last inch, was spluttering and seemed ready to go out at any moment. But its glow lit fitfully a strange and terrifying sight—a human head that stood on the table just behind the candle and fixed the three boys with a glassy stare!

Behind the head, propped on a mound of cushions on a high-backed chair, sat the leader of the Great Council, the Hedtwed—a long-nosed man with a huge white beard and great floppy cap, like an outsized beret. Dimly the boys could distinguish the forms of four other men, ranged two on each side of him, their second heads standing, dark and menacing, in front of them.

The whole council chamber was in a state of pandemonium. The Hedtwed was banging on the table with his gavel and he seemed to be shouting, though no words could be heard over the hubbub below where voices were loudly crying, 'Candles! Bring candles!' and again, 'The storeroom is empty! There *are* no candles!' And then there was a great cry 'Arrest the storekeeper!' and much more shouting and scuffling.

'Well,' said David, 'It's no use bowing to the Hedtwed—I shouldn't think he can even *see* us and I'm certain that if we say anything he can't hear us. This row is deafening.'

'They're going to be so mad about this candle business,'

muttered Toby, 'that when they get around to our case they'll probably shoot us right away.'

There was a gloomy silence. Then Arif said excitedly: 'David, you said the noise must make the Tweds deaf to anything we say. I agree. I do not think they will hear us even if we shout. But perhaps they would hear a different kind of noise . . .' and almost at once an eerie, shivery, high-pitched, wailing note sounded through the council chamber—the mysterious sound of Arif's snake-charmer's pipe.

The hubbub ceased as if by magic and as a frightened silence settled over the council chamber, Arif whispered to David, 'I have another idea—listen . . .'

'Don't stop to explain it,' said David. 'Go right ahead and try it out. They can't do worse than shoot us! And we've been promised that, anyway.'

The Hedtwed was craning his neck towards the source of the sound, and as he did so Arif called in a loud voice, 'O great and noble Hedtwed and revered members of the Great Council of the Tweds of Urrayria; we come to bring you light for your labours. Behold!'

And a great murmur of awe was heard from the crowded council chamber as, in place of the pipe, a gleam of white light appeared between Arif's hands. It grew and grew until it was a large, glowing ball of radiance that lit the whole vast chamber. Then Arif released it and it floated gently up and away to the peak of the vaulted roof, where it rested, swaying gently.

The Hedtwed banged his gavel and the murmuring ceased.

'Much, much better than candles!' he commented, and all the Tweds nodded. 'The Great Council graciously consent to be pleased. We trust your fee for this illumination will be reasonable?'

And Arif answered, 'There is no charge, O noble Hedtwed. Let the light burn there for ever as a mark of our deep esteem for the learned Tweds, whose wisdom we have heard of far across the world.'

'Oh, spare our blushes,' said the Hedtwed coyly. 'Hear what he says, Fredericus, Edwardus, Roseus, Jedidiah?'

And the other Tweds wriggled their shoulders and looked embarrassed but pleased. 'I take it that you, sir, and your two companions are strangers to Urrayria?' he added.

But before Arif could answer a loud, ugly, grating voice just below them cried out, 'Strangers they are indeed, Hedtwed! They stole mysteriously into our city yesterday although the gates were locked and bolted. They have broken the law against visiting the city and I claim the reward for finding them and bringing them to justice.'

'It's Beetle-brows,' said Toby disgustedly. 'Arif had got their minds right away from this business of shooting us and now that man's ruined it all!'

David didn't comment because at that moment he was kneeling on the floor having a quiet hissing conversation with Lord Wrigley. When he stood up he just had time to tell Arif, 'Lord Wrigley says he's going exploring,' before the Hedtwed, after consulting his colleagues, spoke again to Arif.

'Oh dear,' he said, 'I'd forgotten. Now you're here, of course, there's no excuse for not carrying out yesterday's law. We'll have to shoot you, I'm afraid. Pity, you know. Another five minutes and we'd have changed our heads and changed the law as well. No ill-feeling of course. Just the way things are. It was most kind of you to provide this magnificent lamp and I trust you will realise that we are not ungrateful. May I take it that you are quite ready to face the bowmen?'

'Of course, noble sir, of course,' cried Arif heartily, while both David and Toby stared at him in astonishment. 'We are quite prepared to die. Our only regret will be that this event will plunge you into gloom.'

'Oh, come now!' replied the Hedtwed. 'We quite like you and we'd be sorry to lose you. But I hardly think you could say we'll be plunged into gloom about it!'

'I do not speak of sorrow,' said Arif. 'I speak of that light up there,' and he pointed to the brightly shining globe among the rafters. 'As soon as you shoot us, you see, that light will go out.'

'Oh, dear! I see! Yes, that's bad, isn't it?' commented the Hedtwed. 'Still, much as we enjoy this beautiful illumination, I don't see how we can interfere with the law.' But a great hubbub had broken out among the other Tweds. Clearly an argument was going on and the boys could catch only occasional phrases such as 'You're an ass, Fredtwed', 'Ass yourself, Nedtwed' (that was Fredericus and Edwardus Twed at loggerheads). Then 'Shut up,' cried Roseus Twed. 'Jedtwed has an idea.'

Jedidiah rose to his feet. 'Thanks, Redtwed,' he said to Roseus, and he turned to their leader. 'With your permission, Hedtwed,' he said, 'I propose that we defer passing judgement on these people until we have discussed more urgent business.'

'More urgent business?' said the Hedtwed vaguely. 'Why, is there any?'

'Of course there is,' snorted Jedidiah Twed. 'The prisoner, man, the *prisoner*!'

'Prisoner?'

'The man the Ning spies have been trying to find, then. *Now* do you understand?'

'Oh, *him*,' cried the Hedtwed. 'Yes, yes, let's discuss him by all means. Now, there are three points for discussion—shall we kill him, shall we keep him in prison, or shall we let him go? Now, in the first place . . .

But he got no further for, with a great roar of anger, Beetle-brows stamped across the council chamber, dragging his clanking iron-shod weapon over the flag-stones.

'No, no!' he yelled furiously. 'Carry out the law first. Shoot these people and give me my reward!'

But even as he ended, stamping his great foot, the whole chamber suddenly shook to the clang of a brazen bell.

'Look . . . look at Beetle-brows,' said Toby. 'Whatever's the matter with him?'

For a great change had come over the face of their blustering accuser. As the quivering echoes of the bell died away, his jaw dropped, his eyes grew wide with terror and he turned and tried to edge his way towards the door.

'Guard him!' called the Hedtwed. 'He has demanded justice and he has demanded his reward. He shall have

The ugly Beetle-brows bursts into court, demanding the death penalty for the strangers and a reward for himself. You should have seen his face a few minutes later! Or perhaps not . . . it looked even more repulsive.

them both.' And two soldiers stepped forward and seized the man.

Then the whole group of Tweds stood up and the Hedtwed, a broad smile on his face, spoke again to the three boys.

'It is my duty to tell you,' he said, 'that owing to pressure of other business, the Council were unable to find time to deal with the case against you under the law of yesterday regarding the shooting of visitors. The Great Council will now examine yesterday's laws from a different point of view,' and with this every man of the Tweds raised his right hand to his head, gave it a kind of twirl, and off came the head and was replaced in a twinkling by the one on the table.

'The Great Council is now in session once more,' announced the Hedtwed and, as they all sat down, he added, 'and the first thing is to deal with the law about visitors. What do my fellow Tweds think of it?'

'Too harsh,' said Roseus Twed. 'Can't think why we ever passed it.'

'Could do a lot of damage, that law,' added Fredericus. 'Keep tourists away. Ruin the poor shopkeepers.'

'Just think of it,' put in Jedidiah with a shudder. 'We might even have shot these charming people who fixed up this excellent lighting system for us!'

'Free of charge, too,' pointed out Edwardus Twed.

'Well, we all seem to be in agreement,' said the Hedtwed. 'Can I take it that the Great Council wish to throw that law out and go back to the good old law of welcoming all visitors? No objections? Then so be it.' And he banged his gavel on the table.

Then Jedidiah Twed spoke. 'Under the old law,' he said, 'there was a reward for people who brought any strangers before the Council and denounced them. We have a claimant here . . .' and he pointed towards Beetlebrows.

'Oh, that clause goes out, of course, under the law of welcome,' declared the Hedtwed. 'It says here' (and he began to read) '*any citizen who fails to treat a visitor with friendliness and courtesy shall receive fifty strokes of a birch rod.* Take that man away, then,' added the Hedtwed, pointing to the cowering Beetle-brows, 'and give him his reward!'

'Arif,' said David happily as Beetle-brows was dragged away howling, 'you've won—hands down!' and 'Jolly clever!' said Toby admiringly. Arif beamed with pleasure.

Then the Hedtwed turned to address the three boys. But he never had a chance to utter a word for, from somewhere far below the council chamber, there began a banging and a clanking and a muffled shouting. The shouting came nearer and nearer and they could distinguish words: 'The jailer! The Head Jailer! Ho! A tragedy! A catastrophe!'

And suddenly the Head Jailer himself was in the council chamber. He was a tall man, with a big round body on long, thin legs. A heavy steel chain was round his waist and enormous iron keys dangled and jangled from every link. His long arms were waving. He ran up to the table in front of the Hedtwed and he shouted wildly:

'The prisoner, O noble Hedtwed, the prisoner! The prisoner has gone. His cell is empty. *The King of the Nings has escaped!*'

CHAPTER 9

THE STRANGE BEAST OF MUDL

THERE was a great gasp in the council chamber. The Hedtwed called in a loud voice, 'Silence! The Council of the Tweds will deliberate and decide what to do. Captain of the Guard, come forward and await your orders.' And the five Tweds drew their chairs close together and began whispering in a very agitated way.

The boys were excited, too, but for a different reason. 'The King of the Nings!' said David. 'He must be the king we have to find and restore to his throne!'

'Yes, and we'll have to do something quickly,' Toby

said, 'because the Tweds will be on his trail as soon as they've laid their plans.'

And Arif broke in, 'That was why the Nings were sending spies into the city—to try to find out where the Tweds were hiding him.'

Lord Wrigley came slithering up the wooden steps and into the dock and began hissing furiously. Then, at the council table, the Hedtwed suddenly rose and pointed a bony finger at the three boys.

'These people must be spies of the Nings!' he roared. 'Change your heads, brother Tweds, that we may suspend the law of welcome and put them to the torture.' And to the guard he cried, 'To the cells with them, while we decide their fate!'

The Captain of the Guard and a group of mail-clad soldiers swung towards the dock.

'Arif! Boy! Boy! Don't lose your head!' Lord Wrigley was hissing. 'Have I spent years of teaching you magic for nothing? The Head Vanishing, boy! The Ball of Light! Then follow me!'

Arif swung to face the Tweds and his hands began to move in a strange way. Suddenly there was a loud *phut* . . . then *phut, phut, phut*. And then: 'Where's my other head?' yelled the Hedtwed, in a panic.

'Mine's gone, too!' cried the rest, one after another. 'Help! Captain of the Guard! Help!' they all shouted.

The soldiers were bewildered. They wavered. Then they turned and dashed back to help the Tweds, who by now were crawling about under the council table, looking for their vanished heads.

'Now—after me, and don't forget the light,' hissed the cobra. And he slithered down the wooden steps with the three boys at the tip of his tail. He kept close to the walls and glided quickly from one patch of shadow to another until finally they found themselves turning behind a screen. Here a narrow stone staircase led down into darkness. Arif gave a last glance into the council chamber, raised an arm and pointed to the great globe of light glowing in the rafters. At once, as if he had pressed a switch, the light went out, leaving the Great Council of the Tweds, the soldiers and the council officials shouting in panic and falling over each other in the blackness.

The steps went down and down. Soon the air grew cold and damp and the walls ran with moisture. Lord Wrigley would not let Arif make a light in case the soldiers were on their trail. They paused a moment as the steps suddenly ended and Lord Wrigley hissed, 'I came down here when I was exploring this afternoon. Round the corner there is light, a strange room, a strange beast and someone you know.'

'Someone we know?' asked Toby.

'Someone you have met anyway,' said Lord Wrigley irritably. 'He seemed to be friendly. I thought he might be able to help us to escape. But he might be afraid of me,' added the cobra, 'so you'll have to handle this on your own. Besides, I'm tired. My basket, boy.' And as Arif held the basket towards him, the cobra coiled himself comfortably inside and pulled down the lid.

'It sounds very queer,' said David, suspiciously.

'And dangerous,' said Toby. 'I don't like that bit about a strange beast. It's probably afraid of . . . of . . . *snakes*,' (he whispered that word, with a quick look at Lord Wrigley's basket), 'but it might eat *people*.'

'Yes, indeed,' said Arif. 'It may well be a very unfriendly animal.'

But David had been weighing up the situation. 'It *might* be dangerous for us to go forward,' he said, 'but it'll be a jolly sight more dangerous to go back. So come on.' And they all three went on—not very quickly but then of course, it *was* pretty dark in the passage.

Well, they turned the corner and they saw a glow ahead and finally the passage ended and they found they were looking into a very strange 'room', as Lord Wrigley had called it, a very strange room indeed.

It was a round, high cave, all aglow with a curious pink light. This light seemed to come from thousands of mushroom-like plants that filled all the cracks in the rock, right up the curving walls and across the high, domed roof. Over at the other side of the cave there was a great high door. Near to this were the iron bars of a huge cage, like you see at the zoo, and behind these bars they got a glimpse of the curved back of some strange animal—only a glimpse, because there was a great deal of fresh straw in the cage and a man with a fork was tossing it about.

'But I know who that is!' exclaimed Toby suddenly.

The man had backed out of the cage now and locked the gate and as he heard Toby's voice he turned round and saw the three of them. 'Well, well, well!' said the Basket-man. 'If it isn't my young friends! So they *didn't* shoot you after all, I'm glad to see.'

'No,' replied Toby, 'but now they want to tor . . .' He was going to say 'torture us' (Toby's not always awfully alert, sometimes). But David trod on his toe and put in loudly, 'Now they want us to tour the city. And so we asked where we could find you, because we wanted to see you first of all.'

'To thank you for being so kind to us. sir,' said Arif.

'And specially for the bread and milk,' added Toby, who now began to understand what was going on.

'Not at all, not at all,' said the Basket-man politely. 'But I shall be glad to hear what happened in the council chamber. As Head Stableman, you know, I spend most of my time down here. Never know what's going on at the Great Council. Now, what did the Tweds say to you?'

So David told him the story, but only up to the part where the Great Council of the Tweds passed sentence on Beetle-brows, and the Basket-man laughed so much at this that he quite lost his breath and they had to pat him hard on the back.

'That will teach him a lesson!' he gasped finally. 'It's quite clear that the Tweds think very highly of you and I'm sure they would want me to do anything I could to help you enjoy your stay. So I'll tell you what I shall do,' and the Basket-man prodded David playfully in the chest, 'you shall take a ride round the city. It will be an experience you will never forget. *You shall go, all by yourselves, astride the Great Leopillar of Mudl!*'

'And by the way,' he added, 'who's the best sailor among the three of you?'

CHAPTER 10

PERIL IN THE FOREST

'I AM no sailor at all,' answered Arif, with a shudder. 'Always I am sick on a boat. But what is this Leopillar, sir? Is it a fish?'

'All in good time,' smiled the Basket-man, 'all in good time! And how about you?' he asked David.

Well, this was rather a painful question for David to answer. You see, he is a couple of years older than Toby and naturally he feels that he's, well, *better* at doing things (you know how it is). But when it comes to being on the water, this just isn't so at all, because David soon begins to feel upset, while Toby never worries a bit—that is, so long as he isn't hungry. But David is very honest, so he said, 'Toby's a much better sailor than I am.'

'Then that settles it,' replied the Basket-man. 'I shall put you in the front seat. You, sir,' and he nodded to Arif, 'I shall put in the back seat, where there is a place for that basket you are carrying. And you, Toby, because you seem to have a strong stomach, I shall put in the centre seat.'

All three of them looked more puzzled than ever at this and the Basket-man laughed and said, 'It's very simple, really. The Leopillar of Mudl is a caterpillar. He is a lion among caterpillars—the biggest in the whole world!'

'But . . . but . . . but . . .' asked Toby, 'what's this got to do with being seasick?'

'Why, surely you know how caterpillars walk?' said the Basket-man in surprise. 'First they sort of walk up towards their head with their back feet, so that they have a big, high loop in the middle. Then they move forward on their front feet—you *must* have noticed that? When Leo is moving, the hump in the middle is sometimes about ten feet in the air, so if you sit there you find yourself going up and down as if you were in a boat being tossed on the crest of waves ten feet high.'

David looked very much relieved that he wasn't riding in the middle, while Arif turned rather green at the very thought of the tossing about. But Toby was overjoyed. He said. 'Oh, boy!' in sheer delight.

'It gets a bit rough, you know, when he gallops,' said the Basket-man, warningly, but all Toby did was to jig up and down impatiently and say, 'Let's get going!' The Basket-man went over to the door of the cage and unlocked it. 'Come along, Leo!' he called. 'Come on . . . *walkies*!'

There was a sudden stirring under the great pile of straw and suddenly there came through the doorway the huge head of the Leopillar—and a frightening sight it was! You know how an ordinary caterpillar's head seems to be all eyes? Well, the two huge eyes of the Leopillar were like two enormous glowing plates placed edge to edge and sloping backwards and outwards. They were every inch of three feet high—so big that they dwarfed the tiny lip and the strong white teeth beneath, while the forefeet of the Leopillar could hardly be seen at all. As the boys gasped in amazement, the great beast swayed its head slowly from side to side, then edged forward a little further into the cave.

'Bit dozy at the moment,' said the Basket-man. 'He's just eaten about a ton of lettuce—always makes him rather sleepy. But he'll snap out of it when he gets outside. Likes a romp, he does. Come *on*, Leo!'

Slowly the Leopillar emerged, arching its back almost to the roof of the cage. When finally the whole of it was out of the cage, the boys reckoned that it must be quite thirty feet long.

The Basket-man went into an alcove and returned with three saddles which he flung into place. As he tightened the girths he warned the boys, 'Sit between these iron loops on each side of the saddle. Hang on to them! Now . . . all aboard!'

They clambered up, settled themselves in the saddles

and put their feet into large leather loops that served as stirrups. Arif fixed Lord Wrigley's basket firmly in the luggage-holder in front of his seat. The Basket-man opened the high doors of the cave and they saw in front of them the entrance to a long, dark passage. Far, far ahead there was a tiny glimmer of daylight.

'Just a minute!' said David suddenly from the front seat. 'How do I steer? I mean, there aren't any reins.'

'No good with a Leopillar,' replied the Basket-man. 'We tried putting a bit in his mouth—steel bar three inches thick. He bit right through it. Very powerful jaws, like all caterpillars. Just give him a touch with the left foot to turn left, and so on. Gentle tap with both feet together, quickly, for "gee-up". Same thing, only slowly, to check his speed. One big wallop for "stop!"

'And now,' he said, 'are you all ready? Leo will take you round the city walls and back through the city itself. It's his usual evening jaunt—he knows the way. See you in about an hour. Off you go, Leo,' he said, giving the Leopillar a smack on the flank. The great creature moved forward into the passage and the doors closed behind them.

It certainly was a most unusual motion—especially for Toby. Up, up . . . up in the blackness he went and several times he felt his head just touch the roof of the passage. He decided in the end to hold one arm up, so that he could duck if he felt he was in danger of hitting his head. In this way he discovered that there were cracks here and there in the roof, but though he squinted up them when he had the chance, he could not see any light.

"Are you all right, Toby?' called David.

'Yes—enjoying it,' said Toby. 'How are you, Arif?'

Arif was not very happy. 'There is no great motion,' he called, 'but still it is too much like being on a boat. When I see the little light at the end of the passage it seems to be bobbing up and down. I think I shall close my eyes until we are outside and . . .' Suddenly he stopped. Then he called, 'David, Toby . . . listen!'

Far away behind them there came the sound of shouting muffled by the door of the cave. Then, as they turned, they saw a slit of light—a pale, pinkish glow. The door of the cave was opening and the voices grew louder, echoing down the rock passage: 'There they are! Shoot them . . . shoot the spies! Kill the Nings!'

Arrows began to whistle down the passage, aimed largely by guess, for their target was almost invisible.

'Gee-up, Leo!' yelled David, tapping his heels rapidly against the sides of the Leopillar. 'Hold tight, you two . . .'

The Leopillar began to surge forward, arching its back higher and higher as it put on speed until Toby was in great fear of having his skull split against the roof.

Now they were almost out of range of the bowmen. They were nearing the exit from the passage. Outside was sunshine and a glimpse of green fields and blue sky.

And then it happened! A falling arrow hit the side of the rocky passage, glanced off, just missed Arif's head, but ripped the hide of the Leopillar as it dropped to the floor. A great quiver shot through the animal and, in a series of huge loops and stretches, it dashed for the open.

David found himself suddenly out in brilliant sunlight. The Leopillar checked a moment. Then down went its head and David gave a great yell of fear. For outside the cave there stretched, above and below, a sheer wall of rock!

He flung himself back until he was lying on the Leopillar, desperately gripping the iron loops beside the saddle, his feet pointing straight down the abyss. It was then he remembered that, to a caterpillar, it is no more difficult to go up or down than it is to go on the level. And the Leopillar, held to the rock face by the great suction cups on its feet, was not only going straight down, but it was going at a gallop!

Down they hurtled until they reached level ground. David had intended, once they were outside the walls of the city, to stop the Leopillar and let it go back alone while they made their escape. But, although he banged his heels hard against its side, the creature would not halt. Maddened by the pain of its wound, it continued its crazy gallop, heading straight across the wide field for the shelter of a dark forest that stood in their path.

Even when they entered the shadow of the forest, however, the Leopillar continued its mad rush and it was clear to David that they must either leap into the undergrowth or be skewered by the branch of a tree.

'Jump for it, Toby! Jump, Arif!' he shouted, and dived from the saddle, while the Leopillar crashed on through the forest and vanished from sight.

David got to his feet, shaken but unharmed, and ran back to find the others. Arif, still clutching Lord Wrigley's basket, was just picking himself up.

'Thank goodness you're all right,' said David. 'But where's Toby? Toby!' he called. 'Toby, where are you? Are you stuck up a tree or something?'

It was Arif who answered. 'It is no use calling for him, David,' he said sadly. 'I shouted to you many times from my seat on the Leopillar but you could not hear me. Toby vanished from his saddle even before we entered the wood.'

'Then we must follow our trail back towards the city,' answered David. 'He may be hurt. We must find him.' He seized Arif's hand and the two boys turned to run back through the forest.

But what they saw then stopped them dead in their tracks.

CHAPTER 11

THIS WAY TO BE BOILED!

WELL, now we're in a bit of a jam. David and Arif are in terrible trouble (they really are) but Toby was in terrible trouble before they were so perhaps his story ought to come first.

It's quite true that Toby had come off the Leopillar before it dashed into the forset, just as Arif said. But in fact he'd come off *long* before that and Arif had not known about it because he had had his eyes shut.

It had happened, in fact, while the Leopillar was going

along the rock passage from its stable to the opening in the cliff-side. Then the cave door opened behind them and the arrows began to fly. Toby had been lifted very close to the roof of the passage indeed, but as soon as the arrow hit the Leopillar and it set off in panic, its hump reared up so high that Toby was rammed into one of the big cracks in the rock roof. And when the Leopillar's hump went down again he was left stuck up there.

As the Leopillar vanished over the lip of the precipice with David and Arif, the passage filled with soldiers and Toby decided he'd better not try to free himself until they had gone.

He hardly dared to breathe. It was a terrible fix to be in and what made it even worse was that not only his head and shoulders but part of his arms were wedged in the crack and he couldn't get a hand to his jacket pocket. Toby is only *really* scared when he's hungry and if he could have got his hand on those two sausage-rolls he still had, well, he'd have felt a lot better.

Down below, the soldiers at last decided that there was nothing more they could do about catching the Leopillar and its riders. By the time they had stumbled to the mouth of the cavern it was already disappearing into the forest. So they went back into the cave, the great door was shut and bolted and . . . and there was Toby, in a very difficult position indeed.

At one end of the passage was a vertical cliff face, hundreds of feet deep. At the other end was a locked door. Above him the crack in which he was wedged might get narrower and narrower until there was no way up at all.

Toby thought about this and he decided he would wriggle as far up as he could—far enough to free his arms and have a snack. After that he would think again. So he edged himself higher into the crevice and at last he was able to work himself round until he had his feet on one side of the crack and his back against the other.

'And now,' said Toby to himself, 'I'll eat a sausage-roll and think. Or perhaps two sausage-rolls.'

So he put his hand down to his jacket pocket. But in wriggling about, that side of his jacket had got twisted behind him. He pushed his hand round against the rock face, trying to find the pocket. He scrabbled and he scrabbled, this way and that.

And then, suddenly, he grasped something—something that was hard and cold and thick and round: something that made him forget even about sausage-rolls. It was the rung of an iron ladder—and it went up, up into the blackness above.

Gripping the rung firmly, Toby edged himself round until he faced the ladder. Then he began to climb. He was nearly exhausted when the ladder ended against a ledge.

He stretched an arm into the darkness and touched a handrail. Toby clambered on to the ledge and worked his way along it, gripping the handrail. Soon he found himself in a passage where he was able to walk upright. Ahead there was a dim but warm light that grew stronger as he walked along. Then suddenly the light shone strongly on him, bathing him in a pink glow, and he found himself looking through a rock window into a huge cavern. Its walls were covered with row upon row of what looked like mushrooms, all glowing with the strange- pink light. He was looking down into the stable of the Leopillar!

There was no way of escape through the stable door, as Toby knew. So he decided to rest a moment and eat a sausage-roll and as he did so he plucked a handful of the strange mushrooms to examine them. They certainly had a nice colour—but they also had a most appetising smell. Toby discovered. So he nibbled a bit of one and found it was very tasty as well and it went perfectly with sausage-roll. All the same, he decided he wouldn't eat any more in case the things were poisonous, but he stuffed one pocket full of the mushrooms because he thought they might come in useful if he had to go through any more dark places. They certainly gave out quite a lot of light.

It was just as well he had collected them for he was soon in darkness again and one mushroom in his hand gave enough of a glow to see a few feet ahead. But the passage went on and on. Then it split into two and he had to make a choice.

The passage he chose twisted and turned and sometimes

there were little rooms opening from it. Most seemed to be storerooms, piled with old furniture or, in some cases, with rusty old weapons. One turned out to be a wine cellar. Toby decided that the passage must be rambling along under a great mansion. Then he came to a small alcove with what looked like a cupboard at one end. But when he examined it, Toby found that a sort of smooth tube had been cut in the rock.

It came from somewhere up above him and ran downwards in the rock at an angle. As he looked he heard a strange slithering sound. A large white bundle came sliding down the tube, passed in front of him and vanished from sight.

'Sheets and pillow-cases!' exclaimed Toby. 'Good heavens! It's a laundry-chute.' And where there's a laundry-chute, he told himself, there'll either be a laundry below or a place where someone comes to collect the laundry, and in either case there must be a door leading out into a street. And there'll certainly be something soft to land on!

So straight away Toby climbed into the chute and began to slide faster and faster downwards in the blackness within. It was a dizzy ride, for the tube was steep, and Toby came out of the other end at high speed, followed by another pile of sheets that spilled over him as he landed softly on the heap that had gone before.

And then, before he could begin to struggle out, a lid slammed down above him and a gruff voice said, 'Get this lot off right away to the washermen. They'll have to work all night. The Hedtwed's butler wants it boiled, scrubbed, ironed and back again by noon tomorrow. Tell them to boil it and boil it until they get it really white this time . . . if they value their heads.'

Strong arms began to heave the basket, with Toby inside, across the stone floor. He was on his way to the boiling vats!

CHAPTER 12

PRISONERS OF THE HOODED MEN

MEANWHILE, in the forest, David and Arif stood rooted to the spot as, all around them, strange apparitions rose from the undergrowth. The boys were ringed by a hundred hooded figures robed in green. Fierce eyes flashed at them through holes in high-peaked green hoods.

Brawny arms held a medley of strange weapons at the ready. There were stout poles on which glittered the blades of scythes or bill-hooks fastened with leather thongs. There were bows, as tall as the archers who held them, pitchforks with long gleaming prongs, and massive clubs borne on broad shoulders.

Slowly and without a word being spoken, the green ring of men tightened round the two boys.

'Quick, Arif!' muttered David. 'Some magic! Make their heads vanish. That would give us a chance to escape.'

Arif moved his hands in the mystic passes, but still the hooded men advanced silently upon them.

'I try . . . I try,' said Arif despairingly, 'but the power has gone. I can do nothing! My lord, my lord!' he called loudly. 'Come to our aid. We are lost without your power!' And he put up his hand to take the lid from Lord Wrigley's basket.

But before he could lift it, one of the green men stepped forward. Swiftly he raised one arm, and with a lightning twist of the wrist he launched into the air a fine-meshed net. The net spread out into a circle as it flew and it fell over David and Arif, knocking the cobra's basket to the ground so that it rolled beyond their reach.

Still in utter silence the hooded men fell upon the two boys, tightened the net around them, then propped them with their backs against the trunk of a great tree.

Arif cried out in anguish when he saw the basket bounce

and roll along the ground. 'Surely my lord will avenge this indignity!' he said. 'Surely, David, he will rise in his anger and scatter these people with shafts of lightning and bolts of thunder! Watch now . . .'

One of the hooded men had picked up the basket. He shook it. Then he lifted the lid and squinted inside.

'Now my lord will strike!' whispered Arif, expectantly.

The man was about to put a hand inside the basket. Then he checked himself and decided to be more cautious. He turned the basket upside down and shook it violently. Nothing came out.

Arif looked startled for a moment. Then he whispered, 'My lord remains hidden . . . Ah! He waits for that hand . . .'

For now the hooded man had turned the basket right way up and plunged his hand deep down inside.

'At last!!!' breathed Arif.

But the only thing that happened was that the hooded man withdrew his hand. All he had got for his pains was a small pebble. He tossed it away and threw the basket on the ground in disgust. Then he stepped back and joined his companions, who now sat, with their weapons beside them, in a great arc on the ground facing the two boys. And still not one word passed the lips of the hooded men.

'What can have happened to Lord Wrigley?' David whispered to Arif in consternation.

'I cannot say,' answered Arif. 'I thought he was in the basket. Perhaps he was jolted out and is now wandering far behind us. Or perhaps the time had come when he could no longer stay among humans and was called to the land of the Nagas. What shall I do without him?'

'Try not to worry, Arif,' said David—although he felt very doleful himself. 'Lord Wrigley knows some pretty powerful magic and I'm sure he'll find a way to join us again.'

As he spoke there was a stir among the hooded men. Many turned their heads as though they heard something in the forest. David strained his ears and after a moment he said, 'Someone is coming, Arif. I can hear a man's voice. And he's *singing*!'

Before very long there was no doubt at all that David was right. The singer was coming straight towards them, crashing confidently through the bushes and roaring out a song. Soon they could hear the words:

Woodmen, let your axes ring!
Join with me and let us sing
How it is a glorious thing
To be a true and loyal Ning.

'All together, my jolly lads,' roared the singer, as if he had a whole choir beside him, and then he went on:

Yes, it is a noble thing
To be a true and loyal Ning.

Even the great trees seemed to shake as the singer came near.

The hooded men rose and parted their ranks, leaving a pathway between them. Suddenly a broad, tall figure in green, his hood thrown back from a shock of bright red hair, appeared in the opening. He held a huge, double-bladed axe across his shoulder and he sang:

Minstrel tune your warlike harp!
Bowman, make your arrows sharp!
Though now outlaws we may be,
Soon our country we shall free.
Yes it is a noble thing
To be a true . . . ue . . . ue . . . ue . . . and loy . . .
oy . . . oy . . . oooooy . . . al Ning!

'And now,' cried the singer, 'so that the prisoners shall not mistake our purpose . . . the Anthem of the Nings!' He spread his arms wide and the whole concourse of hooded men joined him in this menacing chorus.

There'll always be a Ning land,
A Ning land fair and free—
For we shall pull the tyrant down
And drive him to the sea!

As the anthem ended the singer strode towards David and Arif. Swinging back his axe as he towered over them, he roared, 'Now you have heard our song. Are you for us or against us? Down with the tyrant on the throne of the Nings, we say. What say you?'

Now if there's one thing David hates above anything else, it's being told 'You do this—or else . . . !' And he remembered at this moment, too, that he had promised Uncle Septimus Cobwebb he would see the adventure through to the end, whatever might happen to him. So he tried his best not to look frightened and he said, '*I* say *Long live the King of the Nings!*'

The man in green frowned. 'And what say you?' he asked Arif.

'Leave him out of this,' said David. 'I took a vow to be the King's man, but he wasn't asked to do so.'

But Arif answered, 'I do not desert my friends. I also am the King's man.'

'Then prepare to die,' said the other, swinging back the gleaming axe.

'Oh, shut up and get on with it!' snapped David.

And then an amazing thing happened. The big man flung down his axe, turned to the company of hooded men and asked, 'Well, brothers, have they passed the test?' All the men answered, 'Yes!'

Then he turned to David. 'When I sang of the "tyrant",' he said, 'I meant the evil man who stole the throne of the true King and delivered him into the hands of his enemies, the Tweds of Mudl. You thought we were against the King and you were prepared to die rather than deny him. You have proved your loyalty, so now join us, friends, and let us fight together.' And with this he drew out a knife and slashed through their bonds.

'My name is Merriman Greataxe,' he told them as they stood up and stretched their cramped limbs, 'and I am lieutenant in this band of comrades. Our leader is someone I think you know already. His name,' said Greataxe with a broad grin, 'is *Captain Cobwebb*!'

But before David had got over the shock of surprise one of the hooded men came running to Merriman Greataxe.

Merriman Greataxe strides through the forest singing the defiant song of the loyal Nings. His mouth is opened wide to let all the sound out. The bird on the tree is a different kind of owl.

'Merriman, Merriman!' he babbled fearfully. 'Terrible strange monsters be coming into the forest'—and he pointed a trembling finger—'*a running man bound in yellow rope there be, and a fiery phantom a-chasing him!*'

CHAPTER 13

A TRAITOR STRIKES!

THERE was the sound of running feet, that grew quickly nearer, and soon they could hear someone—or something—panting from the effort.

Merriman Greataxe planted his feet wide apart, faced towards the sound and swung his huge axe to his shoulder.

'Give passage, my lads,' he shouted, 'and let me greet this phantom and its prey!'

The hooded men fell back and David and Arif jumped as two strange figures tottered into sight. The first was a little fat man, babbling with fear. His arms were bound tightly to his sides by thick coils of black and yellow rope. One end of this rope rose into the air, writhing and twisting close to the man's ear . . . writhing and twisting with a strange hissing sound. On the heels of the bound man staggered an even stranger figure—smaller, and glowing all over with a warm pink light.

A gasp went up from the hooded men. Merriman Greataxe gripped his mighty weapon tightly and raised it from his shoulder. And at that moment the pink phantom shouted, 'David! Thank goodness we found you!' and Arif was crying, 'Do not strike! Do not strike! Here is my lord. He is safe!' David called, 'It's all right, Mr Greataxe. These are our friends!' But Merriman Greataxe was already lowering his mighty axe. To the astonishment of David and Arif, he began to speak to Lord Wrigley in the hissing code as the cobra started unwinding his coils from his captive.

'I welcome you on behalf of Captain Cobwebb,' said Greataxe. 'David and your pupil here have passed the test.

Do you consider that Toby is fitted to stand the trials ahead?'

Lord Wrigley finally released his prisoner, who was at once seized by the hooded men.

'My compliments to my old friend Cobwebb,' hissed the cobra. 'Young Hamlet—sorry, I mean Toby—showed great initiative in escaping from Mudl. He'll be all right, I vouch for that. But if you want to know what happened to us you must get him to tell you. I need a snooze and after that a meal.' And with this Lord Wrigley vanished into his basket.

'Indeed, you both need rest and food,' said Merriman Greataxe, 'and that must come first. Then we shall hear your story, Toby. I expect David has just told you who we are?' he added.

'Yes,' said Toby, 'and I'll do all I can to help you put the King of the Nings back on his throne . . . that is, if we can find him.'

'Find him?' exclaimed Merriman Greataxe in astonishment. 'But our spies have already found out where he is, and we plan to rescue him. The tyrant is in league with the Tweds, and they have imprisoned the King in the city of Mudl.'

'But he's not there now! Didn't David tell you?' asked Toby.

'He hasn't had time to tell us much,' smiled Greataxe, and David said, 'The King escaped from jail this morning, just before we got out of the city.'

'Then,' said Greataxe, 'both the Tweds and the tyrant will be seeking him. We must take counsel and act quickly. So—back to headquarters!'

'Please,' said Toby, as the hooded men prepared to march, 'do you think you can do anything about . . . about me being, well, sort of all lit up? And it's not just me, myself,' he added as he drew a tiny piece of sausage-roll, all pink and luminous, from his pocket.

Greataxe laughed heartily. 'You have tasted the mushrooms of Mudl,' he said. 'We know them well. Do not fear. The glow will fade away gradually so long as you have eaten only a little. But now we need your light, Toby.

See, night is falling and shadows deepen in the forest. Walk with with me at the head of our company and guide our feet.'

With Toby's glow to dispel the gloom it was not long before they arrived at the headquarters of the hooded men. In a deep cleft in the heart of the forest there was a great jutting rock. At its foot it stuck out like a veranda over a space about ten feet high and running back far under the rock. Here the boys saw the dark doorway of a cavern. On one side of it a spring of clear water gushed from the rock-face. On the other was a fire over which a cook was turning the carcase of a deer on a great iron spit. In front of this was a long, narrow table of rough-hewn planks. There were long benches at the sides and at one end. At the other end stood a high-backed wooden chair, like a throne, carved with many strange figures of birds and beasts.

And, as they all trooped in, a voice spoke from the empty chair.

'Welcome!' it said. 'Captain Cobwebb welcomes you.' Then, in snake language, 'Wrigley, my old friend'—and Lord Wrigley's head shot up from his basket hissing like escaping steam—'take your place at this side of me, with Arif.' Captain Cobwebb continued, 'David—it is long since you and Toby burrowed underground with the Ugudugu-djuk and found the lost treasure of the Moccasins!* Sit beside them, Merriman, and let us eat and then hear from them how they have fared in this new adventure.'

A pile of animal furs was placed on the bench for Lord Wrigley and while the boys and all the hooded men tucked into great heaps of venison and roast potatoes, the cobra swallowed egg after egg and bowl after bowl of milk. He got so full of milk that when he tried to hiss he seemed to be bubbling like a kettle on the boil.

'Cobwebb, old boy,' he declared. 'I've never seen you looking so well. But you'll excuse me now if I take a nap. Excellent meal . . . excellent . . .' and the cobra slithered back into his basket and began to snore gently.

* In *Captain Cobwebb's Cowboys*

'Uncle Septimus,' said David, 'if Lord Wrigley can see you, how is it that we can't?'

There was a deep chuckle from the empty chair. 'Ah, well, you see,' said Uncle Septimus, 'Lord Wrigley is rather a magical person himself, that's why. And now my companions are all anxious to hear what has happened to you since your arrival.'

So David told all about their escape from the Tweds and then Toby took up the story. He told them how he got into the laundry basket and then he came to the cobra's place in the story.

Lord Wrigley had been jolted out of his basket when the Leopillar plunged into the fields. The cobra had seen that Toby was missing and set off back to Mudl to search for him, thinking he might have been recaptured by the Tweds.

He roamed the streets of the city and, late in the afternoon, he saw one of the Twed jailers about to turn through a door. Lord Wrigley slipped in at the same time, unnoticed. Inside, however, people were just lighting candles for the evening. Lord Wrigley looked for somewhere to hide. There was a basket—and into the basket he went. A moment later Toby landed almost on top of him and in no time at all they were jogging along, imprisoned in the basket, on a bullock-cart bound for the boiling vats of the washermen's village.

'Of course, it wasn't long before I found who was in the basket with me,' said Toby, 'and as soon as we reckoned that the cart was well away from the city, I cut a hole in the basket with my penknife. Lord Wrigley slithered out and wrapped himself round the driver. Then he made the man get down and hold the bullock while I cut my way out.

'We meant to let the man go and then set off together to try to find you. But I didn't know what one little taste of those mushrooms had done to me! As soon as the driver saw me, all lit up like a Christmas tree, he set off for the woods as fast as he could with Lord Wrigley wrapped round him.

'And that's how *we* got here,' said Toby, 'and please

could I have some more meat and perhaps a few more potatoes?'

There was a great deal of laughter about Toby's adventure. Captain Cobwebb's men were a jolly band—not at all frightening now they had thrown back their green hoods. When all had eaten and were satisfied, the voice of Captain Cobwebb said, 'It is late and I see our new brothers are weary. David, Toby, Arif . . . there are warm beds for you in the great cave. Sleep now and at breakfast we will plan our next move.'

'And what of the prisoner, Captain?' asked Merriman Greataxe.

'Bring him before me,' answered Captain Cobwebb. The poor driver shivered with terror when he heard a voice speaking to him from the empty chair.

'Do not fear,' said Captain Cobwebb. 'We mean no harm to you. Have you eaten? Have my men treated you well?' The man nodded his head, still too frightened to speak for a moment, and then he said, ''Tis the morrow I fear, noble sir. If his laundry is not back by noon the Hedtwed will have me boiled in oil, like as not.'

'That will not happen,' was the reply. 'My men have found your cart and are guarding it. And here is your basket of laundry,' added Captain Cobwebb, as one of his men dragged the great wicker basket from the mouth of the cavern and flung back the lid. 'Examine it—is it white enough to please the Hedtwed?'

The man looked at the sheets in amazement. ''Tis like snow on the mountains!' he gasped.

'Then accept it, with our thanks for restoring our friends to us,' said Captain Cobwebb. 'My men will take you to your cart. You can be at the gates of Mudl by dawn. Truly, the Hedtwed will say that no washerman before has worked so well or so swiftly.'

The man was overjoyed and kept turning round to bow deeply as two of the hooded men picked up his basket to escort him to the cart.

When he had gone a little way, Merriman called to him, 'A moment, friend! We hear that the King of the Nings escaped from the great jail of Mudl today. Can this be true?'

The man turned. 'Aye,' he said, 'he escaped—but now, unhappy man, his fate is worse than before. A traitor betrayed him to his enemy and he is now imprisoned in the capital of his own country. *Two days hence, at the coronation of the usurper, he is to be executed.*'

CHAPTER 14

THE MISSING MAGIC

THE news was shattering. For a moment there was a shocked silence, then the voice of Captain Cobwebb said quietly, 'Remember your task, David, Toby? It is to find the King and restore him to his throne. You will have to move swiftly if you are to succeed. Sleep now, for you will need all your strength tomorrow.'

Then Arif spoke. 'Excuse, please, noble sir,' he said humbly. 'May I not help? I would be ashamed to let my friends go into danger without me.'

'We will discuss that in the morning,' answered Captain Cobwebb. 'It is a question for Lord Wrigley to decide.'

So off the three boys went to bed. They felt it would be impossible ever to get to sleep and they began to discuss one plan after another in whispers, but after a time they started whispering more and more softly . . . and more slowly . . . and more softly. And the next thing they knew was that Merriman Greataxe was shaking them and telling them that there'd be no breakfast left if they didn't hurry.

When they got to the table they found that the hooded men—all except Merriman, the lieutenant—had gone off about their duties. Some were hunting, others gathering faggots and many watching the woodland tracks for travellers from the capital of the Nings who might have useful information.

They ate in silence—all except Lord Wrigley, who was

inclined to make a slurrupy noise with his milk—and finally the voice of Captain Cobwebb began the conversation in the cobra code.

'Last night,' he said, 'we left a question for your decision, my friend: will you permit Arif to go and risk his life with David and Toby?'

'You are not afraid, Arif?' asked the cobra.

'I am *afraid*, my lord,' said Arif, 'but I cannot leave my friends to face danger alone.'

'And when you do find yourselves in danger,' replied Lord Wrigley, in a very nasty kind of hiss, '*you* can always get out of it, can't you, because *you* can do magic. So you're not really very brave, are you?'

David and Toby felt furious at this ill-natured remark but Arif answered sadly, 'I have no magic now, my lord. It failed me last night, when we thought the hooded men were enemies . . .'

'Silly ass!' hissed Lord Wrigley, scornfully, "of course *your* magic wouldn't work against a Tenth-Degree Master like Septimus Cobwebb! But you can't have *lost* it. When I drive magic into anyone's head it stays there. Come on, Arif, make your head vanish—that's easy enough.'

But although Arif seemed to make the correct motions—indeed Lord Wrigley made him repeat them again and again and watched him most carefully to see he got them right—Arif's head was still there. It didn't fade a little bit, even at the edges.

Lord Wrigley's own head swung from side to side in bewilderment, and from the way he hissed it was clear that he was thinking and thinking as hard as he could. Suddenly he said, 'I've got it. I've *got* it! Somehow, somewhere, you've started a piece of magic and you haven't finished it off. Whatever magic your mind is making now just keeps draining away to keep the other going. You can't remember any unfinished business? Well, that's too bad. You haven't any magic left. You're just an ordinary boy. Do you still want to risk your life?'

'My lord,' replied Arif, 'I wish only to help my friends and share their dangers.'

'You're only pretending to be brave, Arif,' hissed the

cobra. 'You know very well that you'll have me with you to do any magic that's needed.'

Poor Arif was very upset. But he pulled himself up straight and he answered, 'If my lord will permit, then, I will go without him.'

'Ssssssss!' sniffed Lord Wrigley. 'They won't want *you* with them unless you take *me* along.'

'That's a jolly old thumping lie!' said David angrily.

And Toby spluttered, 'We don't need your mouldy old magic. I bet David and Arif and me can find the king and rescue him and put him back on his throne by ourselves without your inter . . . inter . . . *interfererencing*!' And then, under his breath, he muttered, '. . . old grake in the snass!'

But Arif was aghast. He felt sure that Lord Wrigley would be so angry at the boys that he would magic their heads off or turn them into toads or something equally horrible. 'My lord,' he pleaded, 'do not be angry . . .'

But Lord Wrigley was twisting round until he stood almost on his tail, like an enormous corkscrew.

'Angry?' he hissed, shrilly. 'Angry? D'you hear that, Cobwebb? Me, *angry?* Of course not, I'm delighted, Arif. Cobwebb, I say, Cobwebb! Did you hear him? Did you hear Arif say he'd get along without magic? Did you hear him tell me he'd go without me? Bless my soul, nobody's talked to me like that in seven hundred years and remained in one piece. Stand by his friends, he said! Share their danger! I'll tell you something about young Arif. Do you know what he is, Cobwebb? *He's a real, hundred per cent BOY!*'

And Lord Wrigley unwound so quickly that he made himself dizzy as well as out of breath and his head lay, panting, on the table.

There was a long, low chuckle from Captain Cobwebb's chair.

'What my good friend Lord Wrigley means, boys,' he said, 'is that of course Arif can go with you. You will face the dangers ahead without magic to aid you—all you will have are boyish courage and boyish wits . . . And you, Wrigley, will stay with me and we will talk about old times while we await their return.'

But suddenly, as the three boys began talking together excitedly, Captain Cobwebb called for silence. The boys listened, but all they could hear was a sudden burst of birdsong from different parts of the forest.

'Something is coming and is almost upon us,' he said. 'My scouts have glimpsed a strange visitor but do not know how to describe . . .'

'Whatever it is, it's here now!' cried Toby, pointing.

Right opposite the place where they sat there was a crackling in the undergrowth and a strange, continuous, pitiful, whining sound.

And as they all stared in bewilderment, the bushes parted. Two enormous, tear-filled eyes regarded them. And the Leopillar, whimpering with pain, dragged itself across to David, licked his hand and fell exhausted on its side. All thirty feet of it.

CHAPTER 15

THE FURY OF OGO THE NING

DAVID ran to the spring, soaked his handkerchief in cold water and bathed the Leopillar's brow. Its eyes opened at last and it struggled weakly to its feet—that is, to *some* of its feet, the twenty or so at the front.

All three boys began to pet it and fondle it and the poor beast seemed so overjoyed to have found them that it began to wiggle just as if it was wagging its tail—not that anyone could actually *see* the far end of the Leopillar because, of course, it was about thirty feet away in the bushes.

As soon as the Leopillar had arrived, Lord Wrigley had shot out of his basket and the boys could hear him hissing to Captain Cobwebb and the Captain replying as the two of them examined the animal inch by inch.

'Here we are, Cobwebb,' they heard the cobra say. 'Nasty cut by an arrow. Won't heal, you know, unless we do something about it. What d'you say to a poultice made from *gumbok* leaves?'

'First-rate,' answered the voice of Captain Cobwebb. 'But we ought to bathe it first with some hot juice from a *birgl*-fruit, don't you think?'

'Good idea . . . and finish off the treatment by giving it a good draught of boiled *phazerak* roots. Dug up when the moon is waning, of course, Cobwebb . . .'

'Oh, yes, definitely, Wrigley. Might be an idea to add an infusion of pounded *swozzo* chips, too . . .'

Now there's one complaint about which Toby is the real expert . . . because he often suffers from it himself and he's familiar with all the symptoms. He knew right away what was the real trouble with the Leopillar.

'He won't get better at all,' he declared loudly, 'until he's had a good meal. He's starving, poor thing. He eats lettuce and I expect lettuce just doesn't grow in the forest.'

'The boy's right, I think,' said Captain Cobwebb. 'Why, look at the animal—its mouth's watering at the very word!'

'Good heavens!' exclaimed the cobra. 'I never knew caterpillars needed lettuce leaves! I thought humans had the leaves and caterpillars only got the holes. Leave this to me, Cobwebb. Clear case for a spot of garden-magic. Half a dozen lettuces be enough, young Hamlet?' he asked Toby.

'Of course not!' said Toby, irritably. 'Look how big he is—Leo eats a ton at a time.'

'Oh!' said the cobra, very much taken aback. 'Ordinary ton or metric tonne?'

'What's the difference?' asked Toby, suspiciously.

'Metric tonne's a bit less,' said Lord Wrigley. 'Doesn't need as much magic.'

'Well, I'm sorry, but it's an ordinary ton,' answered Toby firmly, though of course he'd no idea whether it was or not.

'All right, have it your own way,' hissed Lord Wrigley, huffily. 'Come along, Cobwebb. Let's find a quiet place where I can work out a good spell. You can pluck the lettuces as they pop up.'

'Leave the Leopillar to us, boys,' said Captain Cobwebb as the two went off together. 'We'll have him fighting fit for you when you need him.'

So the boys gave Leo a final pat and set off together along the track that led to the edge of the forest. Soon they came out from under the great canopy of trees into the sunlight and the rolling meadows that stretched away to the *pho*, or capital, of the Nings.

Like the city of Mudl, Pho-Ning stood upon a hill high above the surrounding plain. But, unlike Mudl, this hill was a great pinnacle of solid rock. Right around the base of the rock a river had been cunningly channelled to serve as a moat.

A single bridge spanned the moat and led to a winding path, cut in the solid rock. This climbed to the gate of the city, flanked by battlements and set in a great wall, many yards thick, that entirely encircled the rock. Above the wall the boys could see a great huddle of roofs among which there wove another steep and winding path. And this path led to the massive bastions and turrets of the Castle of the King of the Nings. High above all soared the Great Tower, as high again as the mighty rock on which it stood—so high, in fact, that its sparkling silver dome was often hidden by clouds. The boys gazed at the great city in awe.

'An army couldn't break its way in there,' said David finally.

'And if it did,' said Toby, 'the King could be killed before anyone could ever find him.'

But Arif pondered a moment and then said thoughtfully, 'A mouse may go where a horse dare not venture.'

'So what?' answered David, rudely, because he didn't see the point of this remark.

'I mean,' said Arif, 'that it is not always an advantage to be big and strong. If a strange soldier tried to pass through the gate of the city he would be seized and questioned. But who would bother to stop three boys? Who would even notice them?'

'Yes, I see what you mean,' replied David, 'but even if it's so easy to get into the place how do we set about . . .'

'Lord Wrigley taught me that it is best to deal with one problem at a time,' answered Arif, smiling. 'From here we can see only the strength of this great city. When we are inside it we may find its weaknesses. Somewhere in Pho-Ning there are people who remain loyal to the King and some may know where he is imprisoned. These people we must try to find.'

'I know,' said Toby, who had been thinking hard. 'We could pretend we are travelling entertainers and do a little show in different parts of the city. We might end up by saying something like "*Long life to our new ruler*" . . . and watch the people's faces very closely . . .'

'And if anyone looks very upset or cross about it,' put in David, excitedly, 'then we follow him afterwards and tell him why we're here . . .'

All this time they had been striding along among the meadows and now they were nearing the river that encircled the city. Above them towered the rocks and the battlements of the frowning fortress.

And now Arif halted them. 'If we are to put on a show,' he said, 'would it not be wise to stop here—where there are no curious folk to gather and perhaps interfere—and practise the things we plan to do?'

The others thought this was a good idea, and they began to discuss their performance. David said he could do some handsprings to start off with, then Toby could do his juggling, then the two of them could demonstrate some judo throws, then . . .

'But wait a minute,' said David. 'You can't do your snake-charming act, Arif, because Lord Wrigley isn't here.'

'Can you do any boxing or wrestling?' asked Toby.

'Alas, I was taught to be a peaceable person,' said Arif. 'I do not know the art of fighting.' And he put his hand to his forehead and he thought very deeply for a few moments. At last he said, 'Has either of you a pocket-knife?'

'Yes,' said David, 'here you are—but look out, it's very sharp.'

'It needs to be,' answered Arif. 'Come, Toby, and find yourself some round pebbles from the river for your juggling. I will cut a stout reed and make myself a pipe. Let me be the last on the programme. I will play such music as they have never heard before.'

'That's a good idea, Arif,' said David.

And Toby added, 'Yes, and then, right at the end of the act, you play the Ning national anthem and David and I will sing it. Only I've put some new words to it. If anybody is loyal to the real king they'll be too mad not to say anything. Listen, it goes like this.' And he began to sing:

There'll always be a Ning land,
Who cares if it be free?
The man who takes and holds a throne—
Why, he's the man for me!

'What d'you think of that?' asked Toby. 'Don't you think it'll do the trick? Don't you think . . .' But he got no further.

A bony hand gripped the back of his collar. Hard knuckles dug into his neck. He was shaken and shaken until his teeth rattled.

And a grim voice said, 'You traitorous dogs! I, Ogo the Ning, am now going to knock the stuffing out of the three of you!'

CHAPTER 16

ARIF'S MYSTERIOUS PLAN

Now most boys know that if you grab anybody by the back of his collar and press your knuckles into his neck you can make him sit down pretty quickly. But be warned! You can do this only if the other person doesn't know anything about judo. And if he does, what happens then?

Ogo the Ning was about to find out. For, instead of squirming helplessly in his grasp, Toby simply flung up an arm and grabbed one of Ogo's. Then he bent smartly forward from the waist and heaved.

Ogo's feet left the ground as if he had been shot from a rocket, his head went down over Toby's shoulder and at this moment Toby let go his grip. Ogo went spinning through the air and landed heavily on his back.

But the Ning boy was as supple and quick as a cat. In a flash he was on his feet and charging at Toby—a much bigger boy, he was, and heavier, and if Toby had tried to stop his charge Ogo would have sent him spinning. But it didn't work out that way. As the boy reached him, Toby seized him by the tunic and let himself fall backwards, pulling Ogo off balance and on top of him.

As he fell Toby drew up one leg, bringing his knee to his chest. Then in one smooth movement he pushed his foot upward with all his force and loosened his hold on his attacker. Once again poor Ogo was airborne and Toby was on his feet and ready for any further onslaught before the other had landed, spreadeagled, on his back. And Ogo would have come back for more punishment if David had not decided that he had suffered enough and fixed him, motionless, with a neck-lock before he could get to his feet.*

'Let me get up!' yelled the maddened Ogo. 'Let me get up—and I'll pulverise you!'

'You don't get up until you've answered a question,' David told him. 'Tell me this: why do you get so angry when we praise your present ruler?'

'Because he is a traitor, a usurper and a tyrant,' answered Ogo. 'Because under the rule of Andor the Just

*In case you're interested in judo, Toby's first defence was the *Ippon Seionage* (one-arm shoulder throw) followed by the *Tomoenage* (somersault or stomach throw). David's hold was the *Kataha Jime* (one-side strangle, or neck-lock).

our people were happy but now they go in fear of the tax-gatherers and the whips of Duke Urid.'

'And you are prepared to fight for King Andor?' asked Toby.

'To the death,' replied Ogo. 'Let me get up and you will find out!' he added fiercely.

'That is just what we wanted to hear,' said David, to Ogo's vast amazement. 'Listen . . .' And he told Ogo how a charge had been laid on them to find the King of the Nings and restore him to his throne. 'But,' added David, 'the difficulty was how to find out who was prepared to fight for his cause. So we thought,' he added, releasing Ogo from the judo hold, 'that we would sing that song in the city and if anyone scowled as they heard it we would know they were on the King's side. Then we would seek them out later, quietly, and ask their help in serving the King.'

'Then I am happy for your sakes that I heard you practising your song before you entered the city,' said Ogo, rubbing his neck ruefully, 'because some patriot would have certainly knocked you on the head in a dark alley when Duke Urid's men were not around to protect you.'

The four boys sat together on the grass and discussed the situation while Arif whittled away at his new pipe. David asked Ogo if there were many people opposed to Duke Urid.

'All the people hate him,' said Ogo, 'but Urid is ruthless and has his spies everywhere, and a thoughtless word can lead to death. I have formed a band among the boys of Pho-Ning and we are ready to strike if an opportunity comes. So long as the King is alive we have felt that something could be done. But tomorrow, as you may have heard, Duke Urid plans to be crowned and to execute King Andor in the sight of all the people. If that happens, then it is the end of all our hopes.'

Arif, who was trying out a trill on his new instrument, took it from his lips and said, 'Suppose, just suppose, the King escaped . . . would Duke Urid keep to his date for the coronation?'

Ogo considered a moment. 'I do not think he would

put it off at this stage,' he said. 'But what I think he *would* do is this: he would announce that the King had died, hold a mock funeral with an empty coffin . . . and then have his coronation. Meanwhile, he would hunt everywhere for the King, planning to kill him secretly as soon as he was found.'

'Hmm,' said David, thoughtfully, 'and what if the King turned up in the city where all could see him?'

'Why,' replied Ogo, 'then Urid would denounce him as an imposter, a crazy man, and have him slain.'

'This Urid sounds an ugly customer,' said Toby.

'He is the most evil man in the world,' said Ogo, 'and well merits the title of Urid the Horrid by which he is known and hated.'

'What we have to do then, are the following things,' said Arif. 'First: we must rescue the King before tomorrow—the day fixed for the coronation—and find a safe hiding-place for him. Second: if Duke Urid goes ahead with a mock funeral and the coronation then the King must be seen by all the people present to be alive—and he must be got safely away again while an army of patriots is raised and trained to bring him back in triumph. These are the things we have to do,' finished Arif calmly.

'Ho!' said Ogo the Ning with great sarcasm. 'And I suppose you have a fairy wand to bring about all these marvels. But this boy is crazy!' he said to David. 'Look up there . . .' and he flung up an arm and pointed to the Great Tower that dominated the whole of Pho-Ning. 'In the room at the very top of that tower our true King is imprisoned. A thousand steps lead from the tower entrance to that room—and on every step an armed man is stationed day and night. I will dare anything, with any boy,' said Ogo, 'but without magic how can we rescue the King from his prison? Tell me that!'

'Come on Arif,' said David. 'What's in your mind?'

'I will tell you everything, but in a moment,' answered Arif, smiling. 'Be certain we *can* rescue the King. When we have done so, however, can *you* hide him safely, Ogo, until we have prepared our blow against Duke Urid?'

'I and my band will guarantee his safety—with our lives,' answered Ogo. 'But why go on with this . . . this fairy story! You are dreaming!'

'Listen well now,' said Arif gravely. 'King Andor *will* be delivered into your keeping before day dawns again. *And this is how it will be done . . .*'

As Arif expounded his plan the others listened with growing excitement. Finally David said, 'Well, Ogo, what do you think now?' And Ogo answered, 'It is a masterpiece! Let us now plan all our moves in detail . . .' And they sat and talked and went over the plan again and again until late in the afternoon.

At last they parted, Ogo to the city to call his band together and prepare them for the part they had to play, while Arif, David and Toby set off for the shelter of the forest until night came down to hide their movements from the enemy. The rescue bid was on!

CHAPTER 17

GABOOLA THE MIGHTY

THE three boys were in high spirits as they strode across the fields, all keyed up for the dangerous quest of the night, and as they walked Arif played a queer melody on his newly made pipe.

Here and there workers in the fields were turning home to the city of the Nings and one, his dog at his heels, gave them a cheery greeting as he passed. But the dog just sat down, threw back his head and howled mournfully, and although his master called him angrily he would not budge or stop his yelping until Arif put away his pipe.

David and Toby were still teasing Arif about the effect of his music when they came to a place where the field-track crossed a road. A long procession was approaching, headed by a great giant in brilliant uniform who threatened them with a huge staff, crying, 'Get back, get back, there! Do not presume to cross the path of the Most Noble Gaboola! Back, I say!'

A company of soldiers marched behind him, then came a dozen porters bearing on their bowed backs heavy sacks that chinked as they walked. Last, surrounded by a guard of heavily armed soldiers, came a gorgeous palanquin and in it was a man so splendidly dressed that the boys gasped. He wore a coiled turban of cloth of gold, the points of his huge moustache were curled and waxed until they reached to his eyebrows. His glossy beard sparkled with diamonds, as did his jacket and baggy trousers of scarlet and yellow silk.

As the palanquin came abreast of the boys the Gorgeous One turned to look at them. Then he stiffened and barked a sharp order. The bearers stopped and the Gorgeous One lifted a beckoning finger, heavy with jewelled rings, to the boys.

'Good heavens!' cried Toby. 'D'you know who it is? It's . . .' But he got no further, for the man in the palanquin swiftly put a finger across his lips, warning Toby to be silent. Then, with a terrific wink at the three of them he called, 'Do not tarry, young masters. Gaboola the Mighty is great, but he is merciful. Approach and do not fear!' And as they stepped forward, Gaboola the Mighty went off into a mighty fit of silent laughter. Then, holding out both arms, he beckoned them to come closer and closer. And then, giving another great wink and digging Toby in the chest, he whispered, 'So you recognized me, eh, my Glowing Boy, my Luminous Lad? Recognised the old bullock-driver in spite of his fancy rig-out?'

And then David and Arif remembered the driver of the cart bearing the Hedtwed's laundry, his arms pinioned by Lord Wrigley and fleeing from a Toby who was all glowing with the pink radiance of the mushrooms of Mudl.

'It was all right, then, when you took the washing back to the Hedtwed?' asked David. 'I mean, you didn't get into trouble, did you?'

'Trouble?' rumbled Gaboola, much amused. 'Nay, the Hedtwed had never seen laundry so swiftly washed and returned, never had he seen linen so gleaming. Whiter than white, he said it was. And then and there, he bestowed on me the post of Chamberlain to the Tweds for being so . . . so . . . some long word or other . . .'

'Conscientious?' suggested Arif.

'That'll be it . . . what you said,' replied Gaboola the Mighty. 'Just think . . . from washerman and laundry-cart driver to this! And it's all due to you and your friends, the hooded men. If ever you, or they, need help, then turn to Gaboola. He is at your command.'

'That's very kind of you, Mr Gaboola,' said Toby. 'We're all jolly glad that things turned out so well for you. There's one thing I would like to ask you, however. We hear that the King of the Nings has been captured by Duke Urid. If he escaped, d'you think the Tweds would help the Duke as they did before?'

'They would *not*!' replied Gaboola firmly. 'Have you not heard? The Tweds have broken with Urid the Horrid. They have said they will no longer be a party to his wickedness. Aye,' added Gaboola, 'the Tweds have changed since you saw them last. Now our laws are just and merciful. They do not change from day to day. The people are happy and already our riches begin to increase, because they work without fears. And I should know,' he added, 'for it is Gaboola who collects the revenue.'

'And if, O Mighty Gaboola,' put in Arif, 'if the King escaped, we have wondered where he could seek refuge while the downfall of Duke Urid was being prepared.'

'Gaboola, the Chamberlain of the mighty Tweds, can say nothing,' replied the other coldly. Then he laid one finger along the side of his nose, gave a mighty wink, and added, *'But Gaboola, Mayor of the washermen's town of Soodz, will prepare a safe refuge there if this escape should come about.'*

They began to thank him but Gaboola cut them short. In a very stately voice he said, 'Gaboola bids you farewell!' And then, in an undertone, he added, 'Oh, my Luminous Lad, what a lark, *what* a lark!'

And Gaboola the Mighty fell back on his cushions, shaking with laughter, and with a flick of a jewelled finger signalled to his bearers to move forward.

The boys were deep in discussion about this lucky meeting as they approached the edge of the forest. The light was now growing dim and suddenly all the bird-song ceased. Although they had not noticed the chatter among the birds, the boys were awed by the sudden silence now that it had stopped. It was most eerie. No wonder they nearly jumped out of their skins when a frantic hissing broke out almost under their feet—and there was Lord Wrigley, in a furious temper because he was trying to talk to them while holding a metal box clamped between his jaws.

Arif stopped and took the box from him and Lord Wrigley promptly coiled himself round Arif's waist and laid his broad flat head on the boy's shoulder.

'Nearly dislocated my jaw with that blessed box,' hissed the cobra. 'Thought you were going to tread on me and squash me flat. But I had to bring the box. Knew young Hamlet here would forget'—and he flicked his forked tongue at Toby.

'Forget what, sir?' asked Toby.

'Well, for goodness' sake!' exclaimed the cobra, irritably. 'A fine bunch of plotters you are—tramping along in the darkness all lit up so that any spy can see you. Just look at yourself, young Hamlet.'

And Toby, all of them, soon saw what Lord Wrigley was talking about. For, as the darkness came down, part of Toby's jacket had begun to glow with a weird pinkish light.

'See what I mean?' hissed the cobra. 'The glow's gone out of *you*—it wears off very quickly. But I noticed when we escaped from the laundry basket that the light was stronger round your pocket at one side. You must have put some of the mushrooms there, uneaten.'

'I remember now—I did,' said Toby. 'I'd forgotten all about it. I'm sorry.'

'You'd forget your head if it were loose,' grumbled Lord Wrigley. (He seemed to be talking very much like Mrs Green, Toby thought.)

'Anyway, *I* didn't forget,' said Lord Wrigley. 'Keep the

mushrooms—they might come in handy on a dark night. But put them in the box I brought. The light won't shine through that.'

Captain Cobwebb's voice greeted them from his empty chair when they arrived at the camp of the hooded men, and while a meal was being prepared for them they told their Uncle Septimus and Lord Wrigley all that had happened to them that day.

When they came to the meeting with Gaboola and what he told them about the changed attitude of the Tweds, Lord Wrigley began hissing at the top of his voice—almost shouting, in snake-language.

'I knew it! I knew it!' he said. 'I told you, Arif, that you'd lost your magic because you'd started some magic business and left it unfinished. Well, listen to this: one day the Tweds pass a harsh law. Next day they change their heads and change that law and make it reasonable. The day you came before them they had their kind heads on, because they changed the law under which you were to be shot, remember? Then, Arif,' spluttered Lord Wrigley, all excitement, 'you made their evil heads vanish before they could put them back. And since then it's their kind heads that have made the laws, or rather, kept the good laws unchanged. That's why the country is so happy, as Gaboola told you. But you see, Arif,' added the cobra, 'you didn't finish the magic business by restoring those heads you vanished and so all your magic has been used up, ever since, in keeping things like that.

'So now,' said Lord Wrigley, impressively, 'all you have to do is to make the magic passes and return those evil heads to the Tweds. Then you will have all your magic back and of course you'll have no difficulty in restoring the King of the Nings to his throne . . . because with magic you can do anything, and without danger to yourself or your friends.'

There was a long silence.

'But if I do this thing,' said Arif, 'then the Tweds will become bad rulers again . . .'

'And the people will be unhappy again,' said Toby.

'Yes,' added David, 'and our friend Gaboola will probably lose his job and have to go back to driving a bullock-cart and being a washerman for the Tweds.'

'But think how easy it would be to help the King of the Nings with your magic,' hissed Lord Wrigley.

'I would rather all the people of Mudl were happy and prosperous than have my magic back,' said Arif.

'Good for you,' said David, and Toby called, 'Hear, hear, Arif!'

'And I think,' went on Arif, 'that I even want to be fair to that awful Duke Urid. I'm sure we can beat him without using magic.'

'Of course we can,' said Toby. And David said, 'I think you know what we plan to do, Uncle Septimus.'

'I do indeed,' answered the voice of Captain Cobwebb. 'And all is ready—see!'

And almost romping towards them, well-fed, well-groomed, ready saddled and tossing his head in eagerness to get into the fray came the Leopillar. The boys leaped to their seats.

'Gee-up, Leo!' cried David. And they looped through the darkness towards the impregnable walls of Pho-Ning.

CHAPTER 18

THE ROYAL COLLYWOBBLES

HEDGES were no obstacle to the Leopillar, so they were able to make their way across the fields in a straight line to the hump-backed bridge that spanned the river outside the gates of the city.

As soon as they had crossed the bridge they were met by Ogo and a companion, both of whom looked with amazement on the Leopillar.

'He moves on velvet feet!' said Ogo, admiringly. 'We did not hear a sound of your approach.' Then he said, 'From here you must follow the track beside the river until you come to the foot of the cliffs on which the Great

Tower stands. We will come along in our boat here, and wait for you to bring the King down. Then, while David takes this wonderful animal back into the forest, we will row the King and you others to our secret hiding-place. My friend Drogo will meet you on your return, David, and bring you to us.'

The great caterpillar picked its way daintily along the river-bank while, in the shallows beside it, the boy patriots' leader and his friend Drogo paddled their boat silently.

At last they came to the great rock buttress that ran out below the city walls almost to the river's edge. High, high above, they could see the huge tower soaring up until its tip seemed almost to touch the clouds. Light gleamed from the spiral of window-slits that wound around the tower . . . light from the torches that burned beside the steps on which Duke Urid's bloodthirsty guards were posted.

'We'll have to steer Leo between those windows,' said David.

'Don't worry!' grinned Ogo. 'They won't be looking out of the windows. The only way they think anyone could try to rescue the King is by forcing his way up the steps! And now . . . good luck!'

David turned Leo's head towards the cliff and Arif slid from his place in order to leave a seat for the King on the return journey. He stood with Ogo and his companion and, with heads flung back, they watched with bated breath as the Leopillar looped its slow way up the cliff and on to the smooth shaft of the Great Tower.

Now and again, as the caterpillar passed between the lighted window openings of the guarded staircase, the watchers below could catch a glimpse of Toby, on the central seat, as he shot ten feet into space when Leo humped his back.

'He's welcome to that seat,' muttered Drogo. 'I will meet any of Duke Urid's men in single combat—but that I could not do!'

Toby, however, was enjoying himself and he particularly savoured the thrill of being able to see the lounging soldiers on the staircase inside as he went by the window slits.

The men were ugly, brutal, bearded fellows, clad entirely in black. Some were chatting together, others sat in groups on the stone staircase playing dice.

Silently the rescuers passed them and at last Leo reached the parapet of the narrow circular platform that ran round the outside of the tower room in which the King of the Nings was kept in solitary confinement.

The caterpillar ambled around the parapet until its nose was within a few feet of the end of its tail and there it came to rest, panting slightly from the exertion of the climb.

David and Toby slid from their seats to the platform and both peeped through one of the windows into the room. It was almost bare. There was nothing on the floor but a straw mattress, a crude table made from rough planks, and a heavy wooden stool. On this there sat a young man with his back to them. He was writing with a quill pen in a large book, by the feeble light of a tallow candle, and his head was bowed so far over the book, and the candle drawn so close to it, that it was a wonder his shock of yellow hair did not go up in flames.

'This is it!' breathed David and, as Toby moved to the head of the Leopillar and began to fondle it in case it grew restive, David pushed the door ajar and slipped into the room. He gave a little cough and, as there was no answer to this, a rather louder cough.

The young man spun round on his stool and his blue eyes popped wide open. When he spoke there could be no doubt whatever that he was in fact of royal blood. For he said, 'WE are astounded! WE would like to know how the blazes you got in here!'

David put a finger to his lips. The King took his meaning at once.

'WE will be cautious,' he said quietly and he added, 'OUR Royal brain is a little, er, tiddleypush, if We may say so. Have the goodness to enlighten Us.'

So David explained as briefly as possible about Ogo's patriot band, how he had got into the royal prisoner's cell, and how the patriots planned to get the King away to safety while the downfall of Duke Urid was prepared.

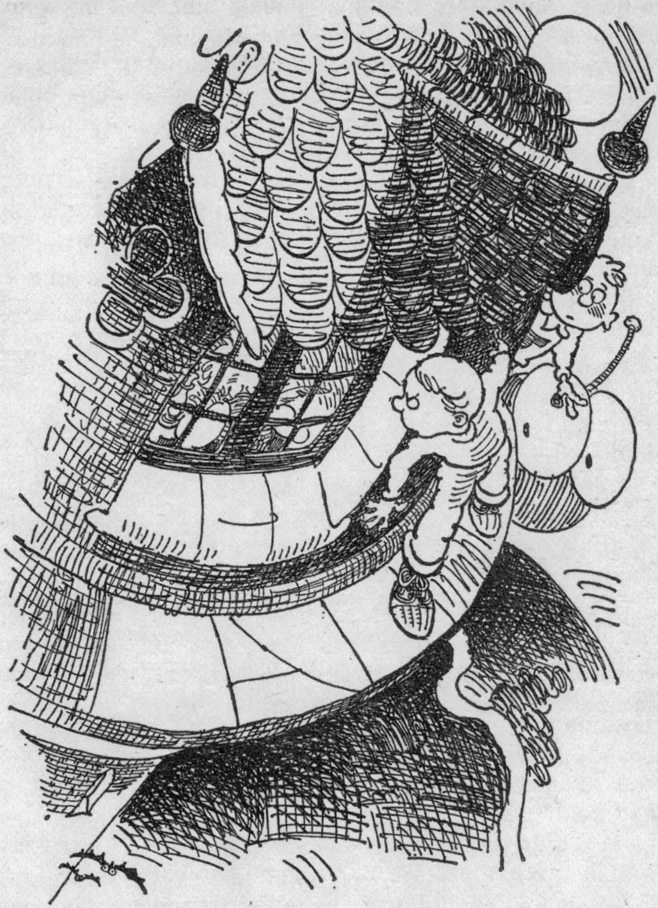

The Leopillar carries the rescuers safely to the topmost room of the tower in which the King of the Nings is held prisoner. Royal captives seem always to be put in cells in castle towers or in dungeons underground. This proves that even Kings can have their ups and downs.

'But time is short, Your Majesty,' he ended. And, trying to remember all he'd ever read in story-books about the way you speak to royalty and suchlike, he bowed out backwards on to the platform outside and said, 'Will Your Majesty deign to mount? Your Highness's caterpillar awaits.'

'Durst pull the Royal leg, sirrah!' answered the King, his eyes flashing. 'Would We ride upon a caterpillar, forsooth!' But then his eyes fell on Leo. 'Forsooth, We *would*!' he said, delightedly. 'Hold the Royal diary for Us!' And thrusting the big book into David's arms he vaulted into the central seat.

Well of course there was no time to argue or to try to explain to the King just what sort of a ride he would have in that seat so David took his place on the Leopillar's neck and Toby slipped the Royal diary on the back seat and sat on it.

'Whatever happens, Your Majesty,' whispered David, as the Leopillar cautiously lowered his head over the edge of the parapet and began to crawl downwards, 'whatever happens . . . do not cry out!'

'Of course We will not,' whispered the King testily. 'WE are not afraid of anything, We're not.'

But a moment or so later David heard a strangled groan from behind him as the Leopillar humped the King far out from the side of the tower and the Royal eyes found themselves looking dizzily down to the tumbled rocks and the snaking river hundreds upon hundreds of feet below.

'WE didn't bargain for this,' muttered the Royal voice, shakily. 'WE think We are being taken for a ride!'

Slowly and carefully the Leopillar looped its way down the side of the Great Tower, seeking the dark patches between the lit windows of the staircase from which the King could hear the raucous laughter of his brutal guards.

At last they came out of this danger zone and reached the cliff on which the tower was built.

'Soon be down now, Your Majesty,' whispered David.

'That is Our earnest desire,' replied King Andor. 'WE

doubt whether the Royal stomach can hold out much longer against the Royal collywobbles . . .'

But the King did hold out and a few moments later the Leopillar had reached the riverside, the King was being helped to the ground and his shaking legs were guided to the waiting boat.

All the boys clambered aboard and whispered their goodbyes to David as he set off to take the Leopillar back to its stable and a monster meal of lettuce.

The wind was freshening. Ogo and his companion bent to the oars and drove the heavily laden boat out into the stiff current. As the little craft pitched and yawed, anxiety came back into the face of King Andor.

But Ogo did not notice this. Flushed with success, he whispered fiercely, 'By Ningo! We have won our first victory, Your Majesty. *And tomorrow we have an even greater shock in store for Urid the Horrid!*'

But the Royal voice did not reply. The Royal collywobbles, it seemed, had won.

CHAPTER 19

A COFFIN FOR A KING

DAVID stabled the Leopillar and dashed back to meet Drogo, who brought him, well before dawn, to the cunningly concealed entrance of the cave that was the secret hiding-place of the patriots. Soon the three boys and King Andor were being led by Ogo the Ning through a maze of passages and chambers that led upwards from the cave through the great rock on which the city stood.

They climbed and climbed and at last the path came to a stop in front of a solid wall of rock. Ogo passed his blazing torch to David.

'Behind this rock,' he said, 'is the workshop of my Uncle Ho, the carpenter of Pho-Ning. This passage will be the escape route for His Majesty when darkness falls again. All we have to do now is to pass through the rock.'

'Pass through it!' declared David. 'How on earth . . . ?'

'You know some magic?' asked Arif.

'WE are not happy about Our being passed through a mass of rock,' observed the King. 'Suppose Our Royal self got stuck in the middle?'

'There is no fear of that, Your Majesty,' smiled Ogo. 'Bring the torch closer, David. I am seeking a small hole in the rock . . . somewhere about here . . .'

'There it is,' David answered as he brought the light close to the rock-face. It was a tiny hole—hardly wide enough to take a pencil.

'Good,' said Ogo. 'Now keep close together . . . and do not be alarmed at what will happen.'

He put his lips over the hole in the rock, filled his lungs, and blew forcefully down the hole. Once . . . twice . . . three times. For almost a minute nothing happened. And then . . .

Then they heard a deep rumbling under their feet. A quiver ran through the floor of the passage. And, slowly and smoothly, the part where they were standing began to sink down into darkness.

'This is how we pass through the rock that barred our way,' laughed Ogo. 'We go beneath it. Now that the platform has stopped, step forward ten paces . . . See, it rises behind us. Now come forward again. When the rock behind us has risen into place the rock in front will sink down.'

And, indeed, the wall of rock before them was slowly sinking and as the space above it widened, a dim light filtered down on them. Ogo blew out the torch and knocked out its glowing end against the wall.

'Come close together beside me,' he said. They stepped forward once more and the floor rose, taking them up into the light.

As it came level with the floor of the room above and stopped the boys saw that they were in a large workshop, lit by windows set high in the walls. Great racks of timber and sawn planks surrounded the room and there were several carpenter's benches, on which tools were ranged neatly. From the shadows stepped an old man, a stout man with a merry face and a mop of dark curly hair just like Ogo's. He bowed low to the King.

'Ho the Ning, Gracious Majesty,' he said. 'Carpenter by Appointment to the Royal House of the Nings, and Your Majesty's ever-faithful servant.'

'Greetings, Our loyal subject,' said the King, who had been thrilled by his trip through the secret passages and the concealed entrance. 'Greetings, indeed. WE are tickled Royal pink by your ingenious care of Us, O Ho. And if the Royal nostrils make no mistake, the Royal breakfast . . .'

'. . . a meal has been prepared and awaits Your Majesty's pleasure,' answered Uncle Ho. 'You boys remain here and busy yourselves at the benches. I will send food to you. And, by the way, Ogo . . .'

He turned to speak to his nephew and as he did so, the old building began to shake to the sudden mad clanging of a great bronze bell.

'Duke Urid has discovered the King's escape!' cried Ogo with glee. 'He is summoning his advisers and the Black Guard. While his soldiers search everywhere he will be planning his next move. Soon we shall know if I guessed rightly . . .'

'Then to work!' said Uncle Ho, briskly. 'Deign to follow me, Your Majesty. No one must see you here.'

Outside, the bronze bell continued its monotonous clanging. In the streets a babel of voices arose as people rushed out of their homes and began to question one another about the meaning of the alarm bell. Then the boys heard the tramp of marching feet. The sound grew louder and louder and there came a great hammering on the door of the workshop.

And then, before Uncle Ho could reach the door, it crashed open. Outside stood a group of Black Guards, ugly and fierce-looking in their helmets of black steel, their black chain-mail jackets and long, tight, black leather trousers. Their Captain, a great beefy man, strode into the workshop, stopped and glared around.

'Ho the Carpenter,' he grated. 'Where is he?'

'He is here, worthy Captain,' answered Uncle Ho, mildly. 'What is your wish?'

'I bring a command, not a wish,' snapped the Captain. 'You are to make a coffin, at once, and deliver it to the Palace by noon.'

'But that will be difficult . . .' murmured Uncle Ho.

'Difficult or not, you will do as you are bid.'

'But,' persisted the carpenter, 'unless I have the measurements, how can I . . . ?'

At this the Captain was taken off his guard. His mouth dropped open, but he recovered himself quickly. 'There is no time for you to visit the Palace and return,' he said. 'But he . . .' and he pointed to Ogo, '. . . yon lad is near enough in size to the one who has died. Take him for measure.' And he turned on his heel.

'A moment, Captain!' called Uncle Ho. And as the Captain swung round furiously, he said, 'I must know what wood to use. Is it to be seasoned wood, planed and polished, or cheap planking, fit for a pauper?'

'The cheapest is good enough for this one,' snapped the Captain. 'So long as the job be done swiftly, that is all that matters.' And he would have turned away again but Uncle Ho went on, 'It shall be so. And now, what of the name upon the coffin? Shall there be a plate of cheapest brass? Or shall we simply carve a name upon the wood?'

'Carve it on the wood,' said the Captain.

'And the name? What name shall I carve?'

The Captain hesitated. He pulled on his long moustaches. Then, making up his mind, he said with a coarse laugh, 'Well, inquisitive carpenter, you may as well know—for soon the heralds will be calling the news throughout the city. Carve upon the coffin these words: *ANDOR. A weakling who could not hold his throne*. Those words and the date—and nothing more. He died last night and will be buried this afternoon. Then shall we crown Urid the Strong, by the strength of his arm King of the Nings.' And the Captain stalked out.

Ogo ran to bolt the doors behind him.

'Well, Uncle,' he asked, 'was I not right?'

'Truly you know the mind of Urid the Horrid,' answered Uncle Ho. 'Have you prepared King Andor for the ordeal he must undergo?'

'He is prepared,' said Ogo.

'And your friend David here. He knows his part?'

'I know just what to do, Mr Ho,' said David. 'I won't let you down.'

'And the costumes, Uncle,' asked Ogo. 'Are they ready?'

'To the measures you gave me, ready to the last stitch, Ogo,' said Uncle Ho.

'Arif will leave later on his mission,' went on Ogo. 'But for you, Toby, now is the time to get on your way.' And he took Toby over to the secret entrance to the underground passages that led to the cave by the river. Ogo pressed on a hidden spring and the floor began to sink.

The patriots were ready to strike.

CHAPTER 20

THE FOOLING OF URID THE HORRID

At noon all the joy-bells in the great city of Pho-Ning began to ring—by order of Duke Urid. Great silken flags of blue and red, the national colours, were hastily erected on all public buildings. Food and sweetmeat stalls, bearing the sign *King Urid's Bounty* appeared in the great City Square and gave their wares free to all who asked.

Paid entertainers roamed the streets and alleys singing songs in praise of Urid. Little flags were handed out to all the children so that they could wave them as the procession passed by. And, amid all the manufactured gaiety, the spies of Urid the Horrid filtered among the crowds listening for any incautious word that might give a clue to the whereabouts of the vanished King Andor.

It was late in the afternoon before Duke Urid gave the order for the departure from his walled citadel. The procession was led by the Duke himself, riding one of the terrible Ninghounds—the fierce, specially bred dogs called the Guardians of the Throne. Horses were unknown among the Nings, the boys had learned, and apart from the slow, lumbering bullock, a man could travel no faster than his own feet could take him. Whoever owned the Ninghounds, therefore, held a weapon of great power. Urid was flanked on each side by a hundred warriors of the Black Guard, each mounted on a Ninghound that bared its long yellow fangs and snarled and snapped at the bystanders as the procession made its way to the City Square.

Behind Duke Urid and his Guards there followed a hundred bandsmen playing martial tunes and, at intervals, the national anthem of the Nings.

And last of all there came one of the meanest of the Duke's servants, the Sweeper of the Palace Steps, leading a creaking bullock-cart. On this, barely covered by a tattered banner, jolted a plain coffin of the cheapest wood. Beside it walked two Heralds who blew a fanfare at intervals and then cried loudly, '*King Andor is dead. Long live King Urid!*'

There was little cheering for Duke Urid. Indeed, at the sight of the threatening fangs of the Ninghounds, the people fell back. But, far behind the Duke and his Guards, the crowds surged forward around the coffin, many weeping and many reaching out their hands to touch the tattered banner in a last farewell. And in the forefront of the crowds were Ogo the Ning, Drogo his Lieutenant, and a throng of youngsters of the patriot band, all tense as if awaiting a signal.

At the entrance to the City Square the procession turned towards the vast Hall of Coronation, in which the Kings of the Nings had been crowned for generations. As it did so a squad of Black Guards formed a cordon across the road, ready to stop anyone following the cart with the coffin as it lumbered away to a burial plot outside the city gates.

But the bullock-cart was making little progress. The crowds were now almost surrounding it.

And suddenly, from the young patriots who were nearest to the cart, there was a great shout. *'Look . . . Look . . . !'*

The cart stopped. A gasp went up from thousands of throats.

For, suddenly, the banner was whipped from the coffin. The lid sprang back. And there, standing erect, in royal silken robes of blue and red, his yellow hair blazing in the setting sun, was Andor, King of the Nings!

'Have faith, Our people,' he called in ringing tones. 'Duke Urid shall never rule the Nings. WE shall return . . .' And Andor leaped into the surging throng of people and was lost to view.

Duke Urid was swift to see how the tables had been turned on his plans to make the people believe that King Andor was dead. Shouting, 'To me, Guards!' he swung his vicious Ninghound around and raced towards the bullock-cart.

But his own bandsmen, panic-stricken and buffeted this way and that by the milling throng of cheering city-folk, blocked his path. With a curse, Duke Urid drove the snarling beast among them, scattering men and instruments before him like leaves, and followed closely by the raging fury of the Black Guards.

But now there came another shock for Duke Urid. For the crowd he was approaching, instead of cowering back or breaking up, were laughing and cheering and pointing . . . but pointing not at Duke Urid, but past him . . . pointing in the direction from which he had come!

Urid flung a glance over his shoulder. Then, shouting with rage, he pulled his Ninghound up on its haunches.

Far behind him, in a City Square now almost completely empty of people, a slim figure in silken robes of blue and red was making its unhurried way into the shadows of a narrow street. Then, with a last gay wave of a hand to the rapturous crowd, it vanished!

But Duke Urid was quick-witted. 'A million *ninglings* to whoever brings King Andor before me!' he shouted. 'King Andor—or his head, I care not which. A million *ninglings*, I swear it. A fortune! And death to any who help or harbour him. I swear that, too.'

And baying fearsomely, the Ninghounds of Urid and his Black Guards swept at top speed into the narrow street that their quarry had just entered.

Now you'll have guessed, of course, that the person Duke Urid and his men were chasing was not King Andor at all, but David. He was wearing a robe exactly like the one King Andor was wearing and his job was to keep his pursuers chasing up and down the streets and winding alleyways while Ogo and his band covered the king himself in a cloak as soon as he landed among them and smuggled him back to Uncle Ho's.

But there was one thing that David and his fellow-plotters had not realised: the Ninghounds could keep a steady pace longer than a runner and, what was worse, once they had got the scent of his trail it would be almost impossible to shake them off.

David doubled and twisted, but the baying of the great dogs became louder and louder. Finally he reckoned that he had given Ogo's band enough time to get King Andor to safety. The street he was in led him back to the City Square and here he broke boldly into the open. Right across the Square he ran and a great yell of triumph went up behind him.

Now he was to put the last stage of his plan into execution. He dashed for the towering heights of the city ramparts and for one of the narrow staircases that led up them. This would keep the Ninghounds in single file—and at the top of the steps he knew that Drogo, who had reconnoitred the ground beforehand, had left him a weapon.

Now he was at the top. And, barely a hundred steps behind, came the leading Ninghound with its yelling rider. But here at the top, as Drogo had left it, was a large round boulder, poised on the edge of the steps and as wide as the stairway. Swinging round behind the boulder David heaved with all his strength. The stone teetered a second on the edge of the step—then down it went! Screams and shouts and agonised yelping told him that it was doing terrible damage among the Black Guards.

David took off at a more leisurely pace along the ramparts and soon he reached the point he was making for. It was an empty guard-house—empty tonight because all the guards had been drafted into the city. And beside this guard-house, pressed close to the outside of the city walls and waiting to spirit him away from the clutches of Duke Urid's gangsters, would be Toby and the Leopillar. It had been a masterly plan.

David reached the guard-house and pulled himself up the ramparts. 'Here I am, Toby,' he called softly. 'Here I am, Leo . . . let's get out of here as fast as we can.'

But there was no answer. For, as David peered over the edge, there was not, in the whole wide sweep of the towering walls, a trace of his brother or the Leopillar.

David dropped down on to the ramparts and looked back. A huge baying Ninghound was just scrambling from the top of the steps. There was nothing to do but run for it, and David turned to do so. And then he saw, coming towards him from the other direction, with gleaming lances held out stiffly in front of them, three soldiers of the Palace Guard.

He was trapped!

CHAPTER 21

WHAT HAPPENED TO TOBY

BUT what on earth had happened to Toby and the Leopillar? Well, when Toby left Uncle Ho's workshop he found his way down the underground passages to the cave near the river-bank. There he should have turned to the right to reach the bridge outside the city.

But suddenly it occurred to him that the river looked much shallower in the other direction and if he could find a place where he could wade across then he could save a lot of time.

He was lucky. He soon found a place where the water barely reached his waist, even in the middle of the stream, and he crossed into a small wood, hidden from the sight of any watcher on the high ramparts behind him. From there he made his way in the shelter of hedgerows towards Captain Cobwebb's headquarters, where David had earlier left the Leopillar enjoying a well-earned mountain of lettuce.

Toby had barely set foot in the green twilight of the forest, however, when one of the hooded men stepped silently from behind the trunk of a tree.

'Have you seen the Leopillar?' he asked.

'Why, no,' answered Toby. 'I thought it would be waiting for me here.'

'Then,' said the hooded man, 'Merriman Greataxe bade me advise you to turn back to Pho-Ning at once and seek some other way to save your brother. The Leopillar has vanished. Our men have scattered far and wide throughout the forest but not a trace of the great beast have we found.'

This was a terrible blow. But the advice of Merriman Greataxe was sound. With a quick word of thanks to the hooded man, Toby turned back to Pho-Ning. His only thought was to get back into the city and find out what had happened to David.

He threw caution to the winds and kept as straight a line as possible across fields, leaping ditches, ploughing through patches of thorn-bush until he came, panting, to the river-crossing. The sun was low as he reached the other side and turned along the bank and he heard from the city the sound of music and the roar of a great multitude.

As he neared the cave he came to a part of the track where a large buttress of rock jutted out almost to the water's edge, leaving just enough room for a walker to squeeze round on the narrow path. But now, Toby saw, his route was blocked. Since he had passed that way earlier a slab of rock had fallen outwards and over it a stream of water was pouring, carrying a widening stain of brown mud out into the clear waters of the river.

Toby began to clamber over the obstruction and as he did so he looked up into the cleft through which the water was coming. His eye followed the stream upward until he made out the dark hole from which it gushed. And then Toby suddenly gave a cry of surprise and set off scrambling towards it.

For the hole was not just the sort of ragged gap that would be made by water bursting its way out of the ground. It was a perfectly round hole, about three feet high. *And it was lined with bricks.*

'It's part of a water system,' muttered Toby, talking to himself as he always does when he's alone and is trying to work out some problem. 'It's an outlet that must have got blocked up until there was enough water to burst a way through to the river. So it should be safe enough to walk up the tunnel now. Yes . . . and it runs in the direction of the Royal Palace. So perhaps there may be an outlet there. Anyway,' said Toby, 'I can't be any help to David from *out*side the city so I may as well try this way of getting *in* . . .' And he plunged into the tunnel.

Well, of course he hadn't got very far before he was in total darkness and it suddenly occurred to him that the stream that was gurgling around his ankles *might* be an overflow from some vast underground lake or reservoir. And in that case he might suddenly find himself plunged in the darkness into freezing waters hundreds of feet deep —alone, far below the earth and with no chance of help reaching him!

Toby stopped suddenly and leaned against the side of the tunnel, his legs shaking. Whatever could he do?

In moments of stress, like this one, Toby's hand goes automatically to his jacket pocket just in case there is anything in there to eat. On this occasion he could find nothing in his pocket except a small box and this puzzled him for a moment, because he'd forgotten how he came to have it. Then he opened the lid and there were the mushrooms he'd collected in the Leopillar's stable in Mudl, all glowing away with a warm pink light.

'Not enough to light my path, though,' said Toby. 'And I don't want to be holding a box when I might need to use my hands scrambling along underground. So why not *eat* a piece of mushroom? It's very tasty and satisfying, and I'll be beautifully lit up myself for the rest of the night.'

So he took the whole of the top of one mushroom—much more than he'd eaten on the last occasion—and he chewed it slowly and enjoyably while he stuffed the box back in his pocket.

In a few minutes he began to feel very much better. He wasn't at all hungry, now, and a warm, satisfying glow was creeping all over him. All over him, Toby noticed, and all around him, too. Great waves of pink light seemed to flow out from him, warm and vibrant, until Toby looked like a great, round, pink Chinese lantern.

'And now,' he said, 'off we go again.'

He had been going for about half an hour when he suddenly saw flickering lights ahead and as he got nearer to them he realised that he had reached the end of the passage and that the lights were in fact reflections of his own brightness, flung back by ripples on the surface of a great circular sheet of water.

Cautiously Toby put his hands against each side of the passage, braced himself, leaned out over the water and peered upwards. And far, far above he saw . . . the face of the moon!

'I'm at the bottom of a well!' exclaimed Toby, 'and this passage is an outlet for the spring when it overflows and for workmen to come along when the well needs cleaning. The question now is: how do I get up there?'

And at that moment, as if in answer to him, there came a great reverberating clatter of heavy chain, a huge gust of wind, and an enormous oaken bucket crashed down into the water in front of Toby with a boom like cannon-fire.

A great wave filled the passage, drenching him and nearly sweeping him away. But Toby held firm and watched as the bucket disappeared beneath the water. He crouched, poised, on the lip of the tunnel until the chain stopped moving.

'Now for it!' he muttered. Taking his courage in both hands, he made a flying leap for the chain. And he made it! For an awful moment Toby felt his hands slipping on the wet links but he gripped tightly and swiftly twisted his legs round the chain as he had learned to do on ropes in the school gym.

Suddenly there was a great jerk on the chain. And, to a faint, distant creaking of the worn wooden spindle high above, Toby felt himself rising slowly . . . slowly . . . slowly . . . up into the moonlight—and whatever fate awaited him in the embattled citadel of Urid the Horrid.

CHAPTER 22

WHO'LL GET THE FORTUNE?

TRAPPED on the ramparts, David thought swiftly as he eyed the enemies closing in on him.

There was only one thing to do—dash into the guard-house, slam the doors and try to hold it against the enemy as long as he could. When he failed to turn up at the rendezvous in the cave, Ogo would be sure to send out scouts to look for him.

So David dived for the door of the guard-house. The Palace Guards shouted and lunged forward. David beat them to the door, and through it . . . but he had left things just a split second too late. Before he could turn and shut the heavy door, two of the soldiers were through, had slammed and bolted it against his escape and were advancing upon him!

Outside, their leader, a tall young man in resplendent uniform, stood with his back to the door and with a very superior smile eyed the snarling Black Guard as he flung himself from his panting Ninghound.

'You come a little too late, comrade,' said the young captain. 'I have just gained a million *ninglings*, the reward that our noble Duke Urid will give to the man who captures King Andor. It might so easily have been yours, had you been a little quicker,' he jibed.

The Black Guard stamped and swore.

'Quite a fight they're having in there,' laughed the other. 'Just listen. He puts up a very pretty resistance, this young Andor. But quite useless, of course . . .'

His joking was cut short by a great, despairing cry. It did not seem to come from inside the guard-house, but from the ramparts. There was a pounding of feet and rattle of bolts. And, as he inched open the door, the soldier within cried, *'King Andor! He's jumped from the window to his death!'*

The captain and the Black Guard leaped for the parapet and peered over. Far, far below, hundreds of feet beneath the narrow window of the guard-house, there was a jagged outcrop of rock. And on it lay a pathetic jumble of blue and red silk—the royal robes of Andor of the Nings.

The captain was the first to speak.

'Dead beyond a doubt,' he muttered. And then, furiously, 'And a million *ninglings* lost to me! Lost by a couple of bungling idiots!' And he swung round on his heel and began to berate the two soldiers at the door of the guard-house. But the Black Guard gave a great roar of laughter as he jumped astride the Ninghound and turned its head towards the steps that led down from the ramparts.

'A fortune lost to *you*, O dressed-up dummy!' he cried. 'But a fortune in *my* pocket. What does it matter if Andor is dead? Our Lord Duke offered a million *ninglings*, saying: "King Andor—or his head, I care not which." Duke Urid shall have Andor's head . . . unless your two feet will take you faster than the four that carry me.' And with a great kick of his spurs the Black Guard set his Ninghound pounding towards the steps and the city gates.

The captain watched him out of sight, then he turned and walked into the guard-house, lifting off his helmet.

'Thank goodness we got to you in time, David!' said Drogo the Ning.

'Thank goodness you did!' answered David. 'I really

thought you were the Duke's men and it was the end for me. But how could you know I was in trouble?'

'Ogo is a careful general,' smiled Drogo. 'He had a watch kept to check on the time of Toby's return on that great beast of yours. When Ogo learned that Toby had been seen approaching from the forest alone and on foot, he put this rescue plan into operation.'

'But my brother—where is he now? Is he safe?' demanded David.

'Alas, that I cannot answer,' said Drogo, sadly. 'He was observed approaching the river, but after that it was too dark to see. The King and the others are safely in the cave and wait for Arif, who is to smuggle the King to another place. But when I left them Toby had not arrived and Ogo was preparing to search for him.'

'Then let's get back to the cave right away. Come on!' said David, making for the door of the guard-house. But Drogo checked him.

'Not so fast, David,' he said. 'How far do you think we should get, with you in your underclothes and that yellow hair dyed to look like the King's, that almost shines in the moonlight? The city is alive with spies and those bullying brutes of the Black Guard. Urid has had to call off the coronation and is venting his anger on the people. Tomorrow the jails will be full. Now what can we do?' Drogo looked around the sparsely furnished guard-house. 'I know!' he said suddenly. 'You must be tired after all that running, David. You shall take a ride! What's in that chest?' he demanded.

One of the 'soldiers' opened it. 'Only some old parchments,' he said. 'Let David get in and we will pile these on top of him in case we are forced to open the chest for inspection. What is our story, Drogo?' he asked.

'A simple and obvious one,' grinned Drogo. 'We are taking the chest to the workshop of Ho the Carpenter to have new locks fitted. In you get, David.'

So David squeezed into the chest and was covered, much to his discomfort, with the musty and grimy old parchments. Drogo's companions slipped their spear-shafts under the chest and lifted it to their shoulders.

'And now,' said Drogo, 'quick march! We must get off the streets before the Black Guard finds that there is no body in King Andor's clothes and comes looking for the Palace Guards who tricked him! A man who has seen a fortune slip from his grasp will not be an easy man to fool a second time.'

They stepped forward, in high spirits, to the steps that led down to the city. But scarcely had they reached the dark and crooked streets below than a great hubbub broke out—shrieks and screams, wild cries of terror and the panic-stricken rush of feet. And above all the uproar there arose a ghostly and spine-chilling wail:

'Woe! Woe! Woe! . . . Woe! Woe! Woe!'

Drogo and his companions stopped as if turned to stone.

'Woe! Woe!' the wild banshee wailing went on above the shouts, the running and the slamming of doors, as terrified citizens bolted themselves in their homes.

David pushed up the lid of the chest. 'What on earth's howling like that, Drogo?' he whispered, scared himself by the fear that he saw on his friend's face.

'It is the Doom of Pho-Ning!' replied Drogo in a shaking voice. 'It is the spectre that appears only when a great calamity is about to fall! Quickly, quickly!' he cried. 'We must get to Ho's workshop and through the passage to the cave before disaster strikes the city and all within it!'

CHAPTER 23

A SPECTRE MEETS ITS MATCH

ON the great balcony of the Royal Palace of Pho-Ning looking out across the inner courtyard, the evil Duke Urid stalked back and forth like a caged beast and talked angrily with his advisers about the events of the day.

In the white moonlight that bathed the courtyard, servants were still washing down the flagstones while two burly labourers sweated at the double windlass of a well in the centre of the yard, bringing up bucket after bucket of water to cleanse the stones and lend a touch of coolness to the sultry air.

And down that well, hanging like grim death to the cold, wet chain and rising slowly upwards with the next bucketful of water, was . . . Toby.

It was the Duke who first noticed something odd about the well. He pointed towards it and said to his Chamberlain, 'What goes on there? The light from the well. What is it?' The Chamberlain had no more idea than the Duke, but the Duke was being awkward enough without having any further worries. So the Chamberlain said soothingly, 'Men with torches, Mighty One. They will have been cleaning out the shaft.'

'Um,' said the Duke. But he was by no means in a trusting mood and as he stalked up and down, plotting further infamy, he still kept one eye on the well.

So Duke Urid saw and heard everything . . . everything from the moment when the well-head became a blaze of light and a great glowing ball seemed to launch itself from the chain on to the parapet of the well and from there into the courtyard.

The two men at the windlass, lifting their heads for the first time as the bucket reached the top, let go the handles with a great cry.

'It is the Doom of Pho-Ning!' yelled one.

'Calamity is upon us!' cried the other.

They let go the windlass handles and fled while the windlass spun wildly, the great chain rattled and the heavy oaken bucket plummeted back down the shaft.

The servants in the courtyard dropped their brushes and backed away, hands over their eyes.

'Who looks upon the Doom of Pho-Ning shall be blinded!' cried some, while others suddenly broke away and ran—ran this way and that, any way to escape the gaze of the glowing spectre that turned its head from side to side at the sound of their voices.

Duke Urid stood transfixed. His advisers melted away, backing through the open windows into the palace, then turning and running down echoing corridors to the cellars to hide.

And Toby the Spectre, the Doom of Pho-Ning, who had had no clear idea when he jumped out of the well what he would do next, found he had had his mind made up for him.

'Well,' said Toby, starting another conversation with himself, 'if that's what they think I am then that's what I'll be!'

He drew himself up to his full height. He turned to face the Duke, who still stood, petrified with fear, his hands gripping the rail of the balcony. Then Toby very slowly raised both arms as high as he could. He pointed both hands forward and wiggled his fingers in a very spectre-ish way, and he began to wail in a most eerie high-pitched voice, that rose and fell like a high wind through telephone wires.

'Woe! Woe! Woe to the city of Pho-Ning! Woe to the House of Urid!' Toby chanted. *'It shall perish!*

'Woe to the Nings who have betrayed their trust!' he went on. Then, as he saw the Duke flinch and draw back into the shadow cast by the Palace wall, Toby turned and began to advance slowly and majestically towards the gate. The keepers fled, gibbering in terror, as the glowing apparition bore down upon them.

'Oh woe, jolly old woe!' screeched Toby, who was now thoroughly enjoying himself. *'Woe to the Nings! Doom approaches. Calamity is upon you. Woe! Woe! What-ho!'*

He passed through the gate and through the outer courtyard. Guards and patrols flung down their weapons on his approach and scattered. Under the great arch of the main gate he went and into the long, steep central street of Pho-Ning. House doors were open for the whole length of the street and citizens were pouring out at the sound of the strange wailing that came ever nearer.

'Woe! Woe! Woe!

Indoors you go!'

chanted Toby and he speeded up his approach, hopping and skipping in a crazy kind of dance along the cobbled street. *'Calamity cometh!'* hooted Toby.

Doors slammed. Streets and alleys echoed with the clatter of running feet.

'Tragedy is nigh!' chanted the Doom of Pho-Ning. *'Dawn shall rise blood-red upon your sorrows, ye Nings who are traitors to your King. O, woe! Woe! Buckets of woe!'*

Toby topped wailing for a few moments. He was rather out of breath and anyway by this time there wasn't a soul in sight. He reached the bottom of the High Street and pranced round the corner. There before him was the workshop of Ho the Carpenter and outside it something very strange was happening.

A Black Guard on a snarling Ninghound had backed three people against the door of the workshop and seemed about to cut them down with his heavy sword. The three were in the uniform of the Palace Guard and two of them were carrying a large wooden chest.

'Well, I've no more love for the Palace Guard than I have for the Black Guard,' Toby muttered. 'But I'll soon break up this little bunch. Here goes . . .'

And with an ear-splitting screech of *'Woe! Woe! Woe!'* the Spectre of Pho-Ning swept down on the soldiers. The effect was all that Toby could have hoped for.

Both Ninghound and rider yelped with terror and fled, howling, up the alleyway. But for the three people on foot it was impossible to get away. Shivering with fear the Palace Guard shrank back against the door of the workshop.

The Spectre was having the time of its life. Closer and closer it came to its quivering victims.

'Woe to you! Oh, masses of jolly old woe . . .' it squealed.

And then suddenly it stopped. Its eyes popped out of its head.

'Oooh!' gasped the Spectre.

For the lid of the box that the soldiers were carrying was opening. And from the box there rose a white face streaked with grime, a white face crowned with a great mass of yellow hair that blazed more brightly than the Spectre itself.

'Ooh, d-d-dear!' stuttered the Spectre, and turned to flee.

Black Guard and vicious Ninghound flee at the sight of Toby, in a blaze of light, doing his Spectre act and crying prophecies of doom against the traitors of Pho-Ning. But what happens when a Spectre suddenly comes face to face with another *Spectre!? David says they should call a policeman—or, better still, an Inspectre.*

'Hey, Toby! What are you running for?' called David from his box. 'Come on, let's get down to the cave. Anybody'd think you'd seen a ghost!'

CHAPTER 24

LORD WRIGLEY JOINS THE FIGHT

DAVID'S companions were glad to put down the chest in which they had been carrying him and they proposed to leave it in the carpenter's shop. Toby, however, said, 'Let's take it under the wall with us to the start of the underground passage. It may come in handy.'

When they were safely below ground they sat down to rest and David and Drogo told Toby all that had happened to them up to the time he pranced up to them when they were at the mercy of the Black Guard.

'He was the man we had fooled up on the ramparts,' said Drogo. 'He'd found out that there was no body under the clothing that David threw from the guard-house and he was out for our blood.' Toby told them about his own adventures in the well, then he asked, 'What are Ogo's plans for the King?'

Drogo told him, 'Arif was sent to the washermen's town of Soodz, where he said you and he had a very powerful friend. Arif was to arrange with this man for our patriot band to train there for the day when we could attack Duke Urid and drive him out of Pho-Ning. When he had fixed this, Arif was to return tonight with two bullock-carts carrying wicker laundry-baskets. In one of these the King will be hidden among bundles of sheets and be taken safely back to Soodz. Who would think of looking for a King in a laundry-basket?'

David said, 'It's a chance we have to take. But,' he added excitedly, 'wouldn't it be safer if Toby walked alongside the carts shouting his "Woe, woe" stuff? That would keep anyone away!'

But Toby said, 'I don't agree. You see, the Spectre belongs to Pho-Ning and the Duke's probably shivering in his castle wondering when it will appear again. But now, suppose the ghost is seen outside the city—and walking away from it, *and* in the direction of Soodz. Don't you think he'd smell a rat?'

With this they had to agree, and Toby went on, 'This is where we come to my idea, and it's why I suggested we brought the chest with us. I think I ought to get into the chest and be taken on one of the carts—that is, if the wood is thick enough to keep in all this light I'm giving out.'

They all agreed to this and, taking it in turns to give a hand carrying the heavy chest, they made their way along the winding passages towards the cave.

Drogo gave them further details of Ogo's plan as they went along, making very good time because, of course, Toby's glow lit up the path like a floodlight.

'Ogo and King Andor are waiting in the cave,' he said, 'and as soon as we arrive we shall all set off by the ford over the river and through the fields to the road. There, we hope, Arif and another driver will be waiting with the carts. The King and Toby will go aboard. Then the carts set off for Soodz while the rest of us go there on foot and by a different route.'

They were now getting near the cave and suddenly they heard someone speaking. Drogo stopped and flung out an arm to halt David.

'That is not Ogo's voice!' he said tersely.

'Nor the King's,' whispered David. 'You others stay here while we investigate.'

They tiptoed round the last bend in the passage to the narrow opening in the side of the cave and looked down. In the flickering light of a small fire they saw the King and Ogo . . . and, facing them, two great ruffians of the Black Guard, their gleaming spears pressed against the breasts of their captives.

'A million *ninglings*-worth of royalty!' roared one of the Guards. 'And a conspirator thrown in for good measure. Tomorrow, brother, we shall be men of wealth!'

There was no time to be lost.

'Come on, Drogo, let's jump on them,' whispered David.

But Drogo, with eyes almost popping out of his head, was pointing to the floor of the cave.

For there a strange shadow was moving, a weaving, undulating shadow, like the edge of waves on the seashore. Then, swiftly, the shadow spiralled up around the legs of the attackers, binding them together . . . tighter . . . tighter! With a great roar of terror the Black Guards crashed to the floor, the spears clattering from their grasp. In a flash Ogo and the King had seized the spears . . . but then they too, with fear in their eyes, were backing away from the fallen Black Guards.

It was then that David leaped to the floor of the cave crying 'Ogo! Your Majesty! Do not strike the snake! Do not strike the snake! He is a friend!'

And Lord Wrigley, still gripping the legs of the Black Guards in coils of steel, was waving his great flat head about and hissing like mad.

'Hello, young Goliath!' he called. 'What d'you think of that? Seven hundred years old and still a match for the best of 'em! And no magic, either, young feller. You saw that, didn't you? Be sure to tell Arif, won't you? No magic. Just mind and muscle . . .'

'But what are you doing here, my lord?' asked David, while Ogo and the King looked in wonderment at one another to hear him talking to the cobra.

'Got bored,' hissed Lord Wrigley. 'Told friend Cobwebb that I wanted a bit of excitement. Told him that if you boys could get through an adventure without using magic then so could I. Remember what the song says,' went on the cobra, very, very pleased with himself. 'It goes: *Anything youth can do, I can do better!* Wait till *you're* seven hundred years old and see if *you* can do this,' and Lord Wrigley gave an extra twist to his coils that brought a squeal from the prisoners.

David called to Drogo and his companions to come and bind the Black Guards. 'And blindfold them, too,' he said. Then, in the hissing language of the cobra, he added, 'Toby, stay where you are until we've covered their eyes. They mustn't know that the Spectre is one of us.'

The task of tying up the prisoners was soon finished,

but the King and Ogo and the others still kept a good distance between themselves and Lord Wrigley, who was twisting around almost on the tip of his tail, hissing praises of his own cleverness. And when Toby came out of the passage, dragging the chest and glowing like a great pink lantern, King Andor just sat down with a bump and took his head in his hands.

'WE are seeing things,' he declared. 'OUR Royal brain must be utterly and completely tiddleypusherised. A blazing boy and a living rope that boils at one end!'

'Who's he calling a rope?' hissed Lord Wrigley, angrily. And David had to soothe him and then introduce him formally to the King and the others. And when King Andor said, 'WE are most graciously pleased that you should make Our acquaintance,' Lord Wrigley was fascinated.

'Why's he call himself "we" when there's only one of him?' he asked David, who was acting as interpreter.

'Because he's a King, and that's the way Kings talk,' said David.

'Hoity-toity!' sniffed the cobra. 'Come to that, I'm a King myself—a King Cobra. You didn't know that, did you? Go on, young Goliath, you tell him that We don't mind making his acquaintance, either. And now, We are going to slip into that chest and have a Royal snooze.'

David, of course, didn't put Lord Wrigley's reply exactly like that. He said, diplomatically, that the cobra expressed his gratitude for this friendly consideration by His Most Gracious Majesty. This pleased the King and it didn't worry Lord Wrigley because he wasn't listening. He was busily exploring the inside of the chest and pushing together a neat pile of parchments to lie on.

David and Toby told the King and Ogo what had happened to them and by the time they had finished, Ogo said they should be starting out to meet Arif. 'As for the Black Guards,' he said, 'we will leave them here for the Duke's search-party to find. And now, friend Toby, you had better get into the chest—if your cobra friend will allow you,' he added dubiously.

But there was no objection from Lord Wrigley. 'Come inside, my dear Hamlet!' he said. 'Come inside and shed your light on these documents. I can't bring myself to go to sleep until I've read some of them.'

Then, leaving the terrified Black Guards shuddering in their bonds, the party set out to meet Arif. It was not long before they heard the creaking of wheels and soon two bullock-carts came to a stop before them.

While the chest was put aboard and the King settled down under cover of some sheets in one of the laundry-baskets, David told Arif what had been happening. When he came to the appearance of Lord Wrigley, Arif was overjoyed and wanted to speak to the cobra right away, but David pointed out that if they so much as raised the lid of the chest the radiance of Toby would be enough to alert Duke Urid's guards on the ramparts of Pho-Ning. So Arif had to be patient until he and his fellow-driver delivered their cargo to Soodz.

Soon they parted, David and Ogo and the members of his band melting into the shadows of the trees and hedges while the bullock-carts creaked slowly along the rough road.

King Andor dozed in his basket. And Toby was dozing in the chest and just on the point of falling asleep when he was startled by a sharp hiss from Lord Wrigley.

'Hey, young Hamlet!' said the cobra, in great excitement. 'I've read all through these parchments. Do you know what's in them? Well, there's a complete set of the builder's plans of the Royal Palace of Pho-Ning. They show all the secret passages and hidden ways in and out of the Palace. And a good deal more . . . oh, a good deal more! *Great snakes alive!*' hissed Lord Wrigley, joyously. '*What fun we are going to have!*'

CHAPTER 25

ARIF, THE MASTER MIND

BEFORE dawn Arif and his fellow-driver had trundled their carts into the washermen's town of Soodz. Gaboola was there, highly excited at having a part in the plot against the evil Duke Urid, because the people of Soodz, who depended greatly on the work they did for the Palace Guard and the Black Guard of Pho-Ning, had suffered much from their bullying and unwillingness to pay for the services they received.

Gaboola himself, wearing this time his simple robes of office as Mayor of Soodz, led Arif to a house that had been set aside for the King and his entourage.

Gaboola greeted the King with great humility. 'We are but simple washermen, Gracious Majesty,' he said. 'Our homes are poor and our means are small. Nevertheless, such as we have, count it as your own.' Toby he welcomed with a great clap on the back and roars of, 'Welcome, my Luminous Lad!' And when he was introduced to Lord Wrigley he was rapturous. 'How lithe, how lissom, is our our noble friend!' he cried. 'What grace of movement! What poise!'

Lord Wrigley almost simpered. He wriggled his head about so coyly that you'd have sworn he was blushing. 'How observant!' he told Toby. 'What a nice chap! Recognises breeding at once. Pray tell him that We are graciously pleased by his perspicacity. Inform him that We are a King Cobra, and that grace and good looks run in the Royal line.'

But by this time Gaboola had ushered them all into another room where there stood a great table absolutely laden with food.

'A pitiful snack is all I can offer Your Majesty,' said Gaboola.

'It is a right Royal snack!' declared King Andor, making for the table in haste. 'WE are famished!'

Lord Wrigley slithered over to David. 'I'm going back in the chest,' he said, 'before I get trampled underfoot in the rush for food. Bring me some eggs and a basin of milk, will you? I think I'll settle down for the night—or what remains of it.'

'How many eggs?' asked David.

'Oh, not many, Goliath my boy,' replied Lord Wrigley as he made for the chest. 'Just a few. Say a couple of dozen.'

From dawn next morning, all day and every day, training of the young patriots' army went on. In the great central square of Soodz, Ogo and his lieutenant drilled their men in the art of spear and short-sword fighting—drilled them to the point of exhaustion.

Alternate days were given over to judo practice, organized by David and Toby. Some of the heftier among Ogo's band at first looked on this as child's play and came in confidently to do battle with their instructors but . . .

'The bigger they are, the harder they fall,' remarked David to his class as he sent one of carpenter Ho's brawny apprentices sprawling with a hip throw—and after a few more experiences like this even the toughest among the recruits had to admit that greater weight and strength did not guarantee victory against a judo expert. From then on the classes were always crowded.

And Arif? Well, there was rather a mystery about Arif. The first thing he had done was to weave a new basket for Lord Wrigley. He and the snake would vanish from Soodz for whole days and when they came back the cobra would be positively simmering with glee.

Ogo once asked David what Arif was up to. 'He sits among the reed-beds making pipes to play upon,' he said, puzzled. 'And I have seen him crouched among the fisher-folk along the river, learning from them how to make nets. He is as secretive as the King is with his secret weapon—as His Majesty calls that plaything of his,' he added.

Now David knew that the King went every day to a small walled garden behind Gaboola's house and that while he was there guards were posted outside so that no one might peer over the walls. He had imagined that Andor merely wished to have Drogo, or one of the other experts among the patriots, give him his sword-play lessons in private.

'I only wish it were a sword.' said Ogo, when David put this to him, 'but it isn't. It is a mere whip. Yes, a whip, such as carters use to flick the flies from their bullock's flanks. Is that a Royal weapon? Yet our King says that with it he will whip Duke Urid from the Palace. Can such a thing be possible? And Ogo flung up his arms despairingly.

'Give a man leave to use the weapon of his choice,' called a laughing voice behind them and, turning, they saw Gaboola. 'Do me a favour, friend Ogo,' he added. 'I will walk twenty paces from you. When I turn draw your sword and advance towards me.'

Gaboola strode away and at length he turned and smiled at Ogo, hands on hips.

Ogo nodded, then stepped forward, bringing his hand smartly towards his sword-hilt. But he never reached it. There was a sudden *swish*, a sharp *crack*. His sword was whisked from its scabbard, twisted in a great arc through the air—and fell neatly into the outstretched hand of Gaboola. Ogo's mouth dropped open.

'Just a bullock-driver's whip,' said Gaboola. 'Long enough to reach the leader in a team of four. Powerful enough, in the right hands, to cut the ears off a highway robber. King Andor is already an expert with it. I should know, for I taught him. I tell you, friend Ogo, he could flick a fly from your nose at forty paces without touching you.'

'I am already convinced,' said Ogo hastily, 'so do not ask His Majesty to do it.'

'Every man has something he can give to the cause,' remarked Gaboola. 'There is Arif, now. But before I speak of him, tell me: why are you waiting to attack? Your men are now trained. What holds you back?'

Ogo grew irritable. 'Oh, Gaboola,' he said, 'you know as well as I do. We lack arms and, until our friends in Pho-Ning have smuggled more out to us and we have made many more ourselves, we dare not move against Duke Urid. It will be many weeks before we can be ready.'

Gaboola chuckled. 'Not so,' he said. 'You may attack tomorrow if you wish. You now have arms in plenty—thanks to Arif.'

'Arif!'

'But *how*?' demanded David. 'I know Arif is clever—but how did he manage that?'

'Because he notices things,' said Gaboola. 'Now you, Ogo, think that we of this town are only washermen . . .'

'Why, what else do you do?' asked Ogo, in surprise.

'Much more,' said Gaboola. 'Many things that the wealthier people are too proud or lazy to do for themselves. We repair the belt that holds the scabbard. We mend the scabbard that carries the sword. We take their armour of chain-mail, clean away the rust and repair the broken links. All day long the grindstones spin, putting a new, keen edge on axes, on swords and spears for our customers. All this Arif noticed. And he heard, too, of the meanness of the Duke's followers—his soldiers and the Palace Guard and the Black Guard, who send us so much work but pay so little. And this gave him an idea.

'Then, as Arif asked me to do, I put on these poor robes as Mayor of Soodz and I visited these soldiers of the Duke. I threw myself on my knees and begged them for work. I said the people of Soodz were going hungry. We would do anything, I told them. We would work for a pittance. And I spoke as Arif had told me to. "Two garments washed for the price of one!" I offered. "For every axe you want sharpened, we will sharpen another free of charge. For every spear or sword brought to a keen edge, another at no charge. Two for the price of one!" I cried. "Two for the price of one!" and so I went on . . .'

'Well, what happened then?' cried Ogo, now all excited.

'Why, I came back,' said Gaboola, 'I came back last night—with twenty carts laden with arms and armour. And when it is ready for return, why, says Arif, *why should not you take these things back to the Nings yourselves—wearing their chain-mail on your backs, carrying their swords and their spears and their axes? And why not ride back to Pho-Ning, right into the middle of the inner courtyard of the Royal Palace, concealed in the carts that go to return the laundry?*'

'It is a masterly plan!' breathed Ogo.

'When do we start?' demanded David eagerly.

'As soon as we can,' cried Ogo. 'Come! We must call everyone together to discuss our plans.'

"'Then, since you are so pleased,' said Gaboola slyly, 'I am sure you will grant one small request that Arif is going to make to you . . .'

'Anything *he* wants to do has my support,' said Ogo heartily.

'Good,' replied Gaboola. 'Well, Arif has trained twenty men to play upon pipes that he made from reeds. He wishes to lead these unarmed musicians against the Black Guard.'

And Gaboola strode off, leaving David and Ogo staring at one another in bewilderment.

CHAPTER 26

THE TRAP CLOSES

ALL through the night not a soul had closed his eyes in Pho-Ning. Urid, furious at the fear he saw on their faces, had raged at his ministers and generals. 'Calamity! Calamity! Is this all I am to hear from you? Would you run away before an enemy has appeared? Are not our troops invincible? Call every man to arms and let me hear no more of this whining!'

So, when dawn broke, the Black Guard stood poised in the outer courtyard, ready to swoop out upon any attacker. The Ninghounds strained against their chains and people in the city shuddered as they heard their baying, for the beasts had been starved for a full day to make them more vicious. The inner courtyard was held by the Palace Guard and its battlements were alive with bowmen and many crews of gunners to man the powerful catapults.

Watchmen strained their eyes, looking out over the roofs of the city, over its outer wall and scanning the great plain beyond the city for any sign of an advancing army. But the army that was to invest the city had come to it in scattered groups throughout the night and was now waiting to re-form beneath the very walls of Pho-Ning itself.

At last there came a cry from the battlements, as Duke Urid paced the balcony outside the Royal Palace with his staff.

'Watch-ho!' called the look-out. 'A company approaches from the west!'

All eyes were turned on the row of tiny white dots, far across the plain. Larger and larger they grew and suddenly Duke Urid gave a great roar of laughter.

'Behold, soldiers, the army that bears down upon you!' he shouted. 'Behold the Wash-day Warriors! The serfs of Soodz are hastening to return our laundry.'

A messenger ran up. 'The keeper of the outer gate asks My Lord Duke if we should open the gate or make the washermen unload outside?' he asked.

'Let them enter,' replied the Duke. 'Give them also entrance to the inner courtyard.' He turned to his staff. 'They come with twenty carts,' he said. 'That means twenty bullock-drivers whom we can put to work gathering stones to feed the catapults. Twenty bullocks—more food for our men. Twenty carts—more fuel for our kitchen fires. And the washermen come with our armour newly repaired and a stock of arms freshly sharpened. Calamity, forsooth!' grinned the Duke, highly pleased with himself.

So the long train of bullock-carts toiled up the hill and into the inner courtyard, where the gates were slammed and bolted behind them. They fanned out and trundled to a halt in the courtyard, while the Palace Guards contemptuously ignored them.

And at this moment a great cry went up from the lookouts. Far below a vast sea of men was surging through the City Gate!

First came a small group, led by Arif. They bore no arms. They held reed pipes to their lips but were not playing on them. And each carried, slung over one shoulder, a great bulging sack. Urid's watchmen shook their heads, mystified.

But there was no doubt about the intention of the disciplined ranks who marched behind. Ho the Carpenter strode at their head, with six of his sturdy apprentices, the captains of Ogo's well-trained band of young patriots. Behind their gleaming spears marched the fearsome hooded men in their green habits, led by the massive figure of Merriman Greataxe, his mighty blade glittering in the morning sun. Near and nearer they drew to the great gates of the outer courtyard.

And then . . . then, everything happened at once.

The gates began to open.

The ranks of Arif and his men divided and moved to each side and the soldiers behind them halted and braced themselves for the shock as the Black Guards on their terrible mounts galloped through the gateway.

Galloped . . . but only for the space of seconds. For, as soon as they appeared, Arif's pipers put the reeds to their lips and every other sound was drowned by their high, shrill, eerie notes.

What next happened seemed like magic. But it was no magic. The hungry, ill-treated Ninghounds had never heard anything like this sound before. You know what dogs do when they hear music. Well, the Ninghounds did just that: they flung themselves back on their haunches and they HOWLED.

And, like so many rockets, the Black Guards left their saddles, sailed through the air and landed at the feet of the patriot army with all the breath knocked out of them.

Then, while the invaders swept forward, cheering, to the gateway, the pipers drew from the bulging bags at their side great hunks of juicy meat and great marrow-bones and put them down before the Ninghounds, walking unscathed and welcome among them and encouraging their satisfied gulpings with more and more supplies of food. The demons of Pho-Ning had been tamed.

Meanwhile, in the inner courtyard, the coverings of the bullock-carts were suddenly flung back and from every cart twenty well-armed men leaped upon the bewildered enemy. Ogo, David and Toby kept close beside King Andor, whose silken tunic, over his vest of mail, bore the blue and red quarterings of the Royal House. Duke Urid, on the balcony, saw his army collapsing before his eyes.

The bullock-cart drivers, wielding their long whips with

fiendish skill, plucked man after man from the battlements, flicking a coiling thong around his ankle and jerking him to the ground. Patriots raced to the abandoned catapults and turned them on the defenders.

'Victory!' shouted King Andor, and pointing at Urid, he cried, 'Let none take him but Us. He is Our prisoner!' And he plunged towards the balcony.

Three bodyguards blocked his path. Ogo swung the butt of his spear against the shins of one of them, sending him crashing to the ground. One grabbed David by the shoulder with one hand, raising his sword in the other. This put him in just the right position for the judo one-arm shoulder throw and he landed on his back in a bullock-cart.

The third guard had his spear flicked from his hand by the King's whip as Andor dodged him, his eyes on Duke Urid, who was now scurrying from the balcony into the Palace.

'WE have him now!' shouted King Andor. 'Follow Us!'

Through the Palace door he flashed, Ogo, David and Toby on his heels. They were just in time to see Duke Urid turning the corner at the end of a long corridor. Although he twisted and turned through one floor to another, one corridor to another, they had him cornered at last. Urid dashed into a room that had only one exit—the way he had come in. And through that door the four avengers came towards him. Urid backed against the farther wall, his groping fingers feeling for the thick silken bell-rope that hung near him.

'You are trapped, Urid,' said the King quietly. But as he spoke there was a sudden sound behind them. The door by which they had entered slammed shut and they heard a heavy bolt fall into place.

'No. It is you who are trapped, Andor the Witless!' sneered the Duke, his hand beginning to close around the bell-rope. 'As soon as I pull this rope the floor beneath you will open. The shaft below is many hundreds of feet deep and the bottom is covered with iron spikes. Goodbye, Andor!'

Urid tightened his grip. But he seemed to have missed

The lash, skilfully wielded by King Andor, sweeps Duke Urid's sword from his grasp. It is now clear to everybody that the King has the whip-hand.

the bell-rope. He grabbed again. And again. And this time the bell-rope, as if it were alive, evaded his clutch and rose up, up towards the ceiling, utterly and completely beyond his reach. And from the end of the bell-rope there came a strange hissing.

'Kindly present my compliments to his Royal Highness,' said Lord Wrigley. twisting about ecstatically. 'Tell him We Kings stick together!'

David's broad grin as he told King Andor what the cobra said was clear evidence to Urid that he had been tricked. His hand went to his sword . . . but he had hardly moved before the weapon was tossed to the far end of the room by a flick of Andor's whip.

'WE are now going to strip you of your honours,' declared the King. 'First, the Imperial Order of the Knights of Ning,' (*flick* . . . and the jewelled cross was torn from Urid's breast). 'Next, the Medal of Honour', (*flick*). 'Now, the . . .'

With a wild scream of hate, Urid leaped towards a large stone urn that stood on a marble table beside the wall. He wrapped his arms around the urn, meaning to heave it at King and crush him beneath its weight. But as soon as he lifted the urn an inch above the table a dark shaft yawned beneath his feet! With a despairing shriek Urid, the heavy urn still clasped in his arms, plunged into the blackness below and the slab of flooring swung silently back into place.

Lord Wrigley dropped to the floor and slithered towards the King, Ogo and the boys.

'I say, young Hamlet,' he hissed to Toby. 'Have the goodness to convey to Our Royal Brother Our confirmation that he is now the undisputed King of the Nings. Oh, yes, and ask him: what about having a Royal celebration party?'

CHAPTER 27

NOW YOU SEE ME—NOW YOU DON'T!

AND a party there was—a party that took in the whole population of Pho-Ning, with tables laid in the great square and wine from the Royal cellars gushing from the spouts of every fountain.

By the time the celebrations officially began in the early evening, the city had been purged of the enemy. Dozens, trying to escape through the maze of secret tunnels beneath the Royal Palace, had found themselves caught in the nets that Arif had prepared and fixed across every exit—for he and Lord Wrigley had made a very careful study of the builder's plans of escape routes, secret panels . . . and especially of the devilish booby-traps, as Duke Urid had discovered too late. Though most of the King's enemies were condemned to prison, the bullies of the Black Guard, stripped of all their stolen wealth and property and of every weapon, were branded as outlaws and scourged from the city, forbidden ever to return upon pain of death.

In the great hall of the Royal Palace that afternoon, King Andor thanked and rewarded his loyal helpers. Ogo and his companions became the King's own personal Bodyguard. Ho the carpenter was given the title of *Bung* (Royal Brother) and it was decreed that all citizens, on meeting him, should salute him with a cry of *Bung* Ho!

There was a great stir when Gaboola the Mighty entered, in his rich robes of office as a dignitary in the service of the Tweds of Urrayria, and announced that his country wished to be the first to welcome the victory of King Andor and to offer him a perpetual Treaty of Friendship.

The King signed the document with a great flourish,

and as he handed it back to Gaboola, he said without a smile, 'WE seem to recognise the name Gaboola. Have you a kinsman of that name, perhaps?'

'The Mayor of Soodz, a poor and insignificant person, is the brother of your even more insignificant and most humble servant,' replied Gaboola, with a very low bow.

'WE are displeased with him,' said King Andor.

'Command me, Gracious Majesty,' declared Gaboola, enjoying the game, 'and I will see that the dog obeys. My life upon it!'

'The town of Soodz,' replied Andor, coldly, has failed to collect from Pho-Ning its dues for laundering, for the repair of armour or the sharpening of spears and other weapons since the time, five years ago, when Duke Urid usurped the throne of the Nings. It is shameful that We, King Andor, should be held to be a debtor. It is therefore decreed that the sum of ten thousand *ninglings* shall be paid forthwith from the Royal *Treasury* to every household in the town of Soodz . . .'

'Your Most Gracious Majesty's generosity . . .' began Gaboola.

'. . . and the sum of a million *ninglings* to this Gaboola, the Mayor of Soodz,' went on King Andor, 'in order to encourage him to send in his people's accounts more promptly in future.'

And as Gaboola retired, to take the Treaty of Friendship back in triumph to his masters, the Tweds in Mudl, and richer himself by a million *ninglings*, King Andor bestowed upon him a discreet Royal wink.

Then, for David and Toby and Arif, came the hardest part of the adventure . . . to say goodbye to King Andor and their many new friends. They had carried out their secret orders. They had found the King, foiled his enemies, and restored him to his throne. It was time to go. They wondered how they could explain this without offence to Andor, who wanted them to come and live among the Nings and help him govern his people wisely.

It was Lord Wrigley who found a way out of the difficulty. He had been having a quiet hiss in one corner with Merriman Greataxe and now he brought that tall warrior to the King's side and Merriman interpreted his hissing to Andor.

'Gracious Majesty,' said Lord Wrigley, 'this hooded man and his companions have fought doughtily for your return since they were outlawed from their country. But they have a duty to fulfil before they return to live once more in their beloved Pho-Ning. They ask a favour of you.'

'WE grant it gladly, whatever it be,' declared the King promptly.

'I beg you to hear me out, before you decide,' said Lord Wrigley. 'They ask you to permit my three young friends—and my moderately humble self—to leave Pho-Ning with them at once. A thing of great value vanished from their camp while they were fighting with your troops and a search is being set on foot.'

'Then go they must,' replied the King. 'How could We withhold help from those who helped Us? When are you likely to return?'

'Who can say, Majesty?' answered the cobra, craftily. 'The search may be long, the trail dangerous. But the sooner we start . . .'

And so, after much hand-clasping and back-slapping and cheering, the three boys—with Lord Wrigley sleeping, full of eggs and milk, in his basket—set out with Merriman Greataxe and the hooded men for the camp in the forest.

They found the great table laid for a sumptuous meal. 'You have missed the Royal banquet,' said the voice of Captain Cobwebb, 'so we will have a banquet of our own. Now eat and be merry. You have accomplished your task. What follows, and why you have been so urgently called from the King's side, you have yet to learn. But for the present: no questions.'

When at last the meal was finished and even Toby could eat no more, and when they had each told of their adventures a dozen times, the voice of Captain Cobwebb called for silence.

'King Andor sits again upon his throne,' he said, 'and my Secret Orders have been carried out. I would have left you longer merrymaking with the King but Lord Wrigley has been urgently recalled to his country.'

'Extraordinary meeting of the Cobra Club Committee,' hissed Lord Wrigley. 'They're going to make me a Life Member—very rare honour for a youngster of my age. So I've got to get back right away.'

He and Arif started saying their goodbyes to everybody and David and Toby and Arif all said they hoped that they'd have another adventure together some day and that Lord Wrigley would join them.

And then Lord Wrigley, who by this time had utterly and completely forgotten their real names, said, 'Now, you, Goliath and you, young Hamlet. We've managed all this adventure of putting the King back on his throne without any magic . . . how would you like me to show you a very special piece of magic? Come along, Arif.'

Everyone sat down in a half-circle, their faces lit by the flickering flames of the forest fire, and all around them the gathering gloom of the forest, for night was drawing on.

Lord Wrigley coiled himself tightly on the grass. Arif squatted cross-legged before him and then, as the boys had seen before, he seemed to conjure from the air his bulbous snake-charmer's pipe and began to play a weird strain, moving the pipe from side to side.

Then Lord Wrigley lifted his great flat head and began to sway to the movements of the pipe. And as he swayed to and fro, he lifted his head higher and higher . . . higher and higher until, to a gasp of wonderment from every watcher, the great cobra was standing rigid on the tip of his tail. And still he continued to stretch his head upwards. It vanished from the range of the firelight, into the shadows between the trees, and at last it faded completely into the darkness above.

And then the music ceased. The pipe vanished from between the hands of Arif. He stood up stiffly, put the palms of his hands together and bowed silently to his audience. Then he turned. He reached up and clasped his hands around the body of the cobra. And, as if mounting a rope, he began to climb . . . up, up into the darkness. And as he slowly passed from their view the snake's body coiled up beneath his feet and boy and cobra vanished from the sight of everyone.

There was a long, long silence. Toby was the first to speak. He said, 'When are they coming down again?'

'They will not come down again,' answered Uncle Septimus. 'They are on their way to the Cobra Club. The call was urgent, you remember.'

'But if we're not travelling with them,' asked David, 'how are we to get home now the adventure's finished?'

There was a great chuckle from the direction of Captain Septimus Cobwebb's chair. 'Surely you heard what our friend Wrigley told the King—about a thing of great value that was missing from the camp, and the search that was to be made?' he said. 'Well, you and Toby are to make that search.

'You'd better be on your way,' added Uncle Septimus. 'Off you go, boys. *Find the Leopillar—and the Leopillar will carry you home!*'

CHAPTER 28

THE GREAT ESCAPE

MERRIMAN Greataxe stretched himself and got up from the table. 'We have searched long,' he said, 'and we can be of some help to you, for we have found the tracks of the Leopillar. I will take you to the point where they reach the edge of the forest.'

So, after a last goodbye to the invisible Uncle Septimus and the rest of the hooded men, they set off with Merriman. They found the track of the great beast but these ceased where the forest ended.

'From here on you must use your wits,' said Merriman. 'There has been no rain for days and the wind has covered the tracks with sand.'

He lifted his arm in farewell and melted into the darkness of the forest. David and Toby walked out into the great loneliness of the bare, moonlit plain.

They must have tramped along for a couple of hours when Toby suddenly stopped and pointed to something that lay to the left of the line they were taking.

'That looks like one of the Leopillar's saddles,' he said. 'Come on!'

Sure enough, that's what it was. And as they scanned the plain around they soon spotted another, and beyond it a third.

'If you were to draw a line beyond that one,' said David, 'it would take you past that big arm of the forest that reaches out over there and right into the middle of that circle of trees—the clump that stands all by itself.'

'I bet that's where he is!' cried Toby. 'Let's go! I wonder how long it'll be before we're home? I wonder what's for supper?' And they charged forward.

They reached the tip of the dark tongue of forest and they were almost past it when suddenly, with a great crackling of undergrowth and snapping of branches, four huge figures burst into the moonlight. They were brandishing enormous clubs and with shouts of evil triumph they pounded towards the two boys.

'Run for your life!' yelled David. 'It's the Black Guards—the ones that were outlawed!'

'Make for the wood,' panted Toby. 'It's our only chance!'

The two boys were lighter on their feet than the Black Guards, but they had already marched a long way and although the outlaws were unused to exercise, having spent most of their time riding about on their Ninghounds, they were fresher. At length they began to gain on David and Toby and they got so close that the boys could feel the ground shake under their heavy tread.

But David and Toby had reached the edge of the wood now and they plunged into the undergrowth. Being smaller and more agile, they were able to put a distance between them and their pursuers, and to do so in comparative silence, while the burly Black Guards thrashed about clumsily and gave away their position with every move.

At last David and Toby just had to stop and rest. They had reached a small clearing, deep in the wood, and here they sat down and leaned their backs against a long ridge of wrinkled rock that looked like a great fossilised tree trunk.

They sat there for hours, it seemed, listening to their pursuers floundering about. Then the voices died away and, after a time, a voice cried, 'A truce! A truce! Call out if you will accept a truce!'

'As if we'd fall for that old trick!' David muttered. 'If we call out they'll know our position at once!'

So the boys didn't answer. And after a few minutes the voice called again, 'Very well. Then we shall burn you out!'

And as the voice died away they heard the crackling of flames. It came from all around them. Great plumes of smoke drifted across the face of the moon and, whichever way they looked, they could see an angry red glow.

The air grew stifling and the rock against which they had been leaning absorbed the heat and grew so hot that it seemed the very stone must break. And suddenly, with an ear-shattering crack, the long ridge split from end to end! And then . . .

'Look, Toby, look!' cried David.

From the huge rift in the rock there began to rise what looked like two great curtains, black and wrinkled. But, in the great heat of the narrowing ring of flames, they dried taut as soon as they unfolded. Bold patterns of beautiful, glowing colours grew upon them, flashing rainbow hues against the pall of smoke.

And Toby let out a great, triumphant shout.

'It's the Leopillar!' he yelled. 'It came here to turn into a chrysalis and now it's hatching out as a moth!'

He was right, and it was clear now, for the great legs emerged and pulled the enormous body to the top of the empty cocoon. The vast wings quivered as the creature tested the weight of its body against their lifting power.

'Look out—it's going to fly!' shouted David. 'Get on its back quickly, Toby, before it takes off!'

Well, they made it . . . they *just* made it. They scrambled to the top of the cocoon, flung themselves into the deep, soft fur of the great moth's broad back and grabbed fistfuls of it to hold themselves in place. And, silently, the moth soared up and up, until the blazing woodland dwindled to a star-like twinkle far away below and finally vanished altogether.

They were so cosy on their couch of fur, the flight was so smooth and silent and they were so exhausted that they soon began to doze. But after a long, long time, Toby stirred and said sleepily, 'I say, David, when a Leopillar changes into a moth, what d'you call it then? D'you think it's a Leomoth? David, I say, David! What do *you* think we ought to call it?'

But the voice that answered wasn't David's.

'Oh, the poor things!' said Mrs Green. 'Huddled up on the doorstep half asleep! Oh, I *am* sorry to be so late, boys.'

'Well, you know how your Aunt Christabel talks,' said Mr Green. 'Come along, my jolly lads, in you go. A nice hot bath, some supper and then off to bed. You look tired out.'

And he was right. They were so tired that Toby didn't even ask for second helpings.

When at last they'd clambered into bed and were snuggling down Mrs Green said, 'What have you been doing with yourselves all day?'

Now, as you know, the proper answer to this question is 'Nothing'. But David was tired and therefore not quite as alert as he usually is. So he told her. He said, 'Well, we rescued the King of the Nings from prison and restored him to his throne.'

And Toby said, 'I'll sing you a bit of the patriots' battle-song, if you like. It goes like this:

O, we will build a Ning land free
Where none shall sigh nor moan,
Where every Ning has a Ninglenook
In a Nouse and a Nome of his own.

With ninglings jingling in his purse
A Nappy man he'll be,
And in his garden he'll keep a Nen
To lay him a Negg for his tea.

And there is something more besides
Each Ning will have, of course, . . .'

But we'll probably never learn what other thing it is that every Ning will have because at this point Mrs Green started laughing and interrupted him. 'Go to sleep, Toby!' she said. 'Really, what a lot of rubbish you boys do talk!' And she switched off the light and went downstairs.

Well, there you are, you see—that's the way it is with grown-ups. When you *do* tell them they don't believe you.